Satchmo

GARY GIDDINS

Satchmo

The Genius of
LOUIS ARMSTRONG

DA CAPO PRESS

A CIP catalog record for this book is available from the Library of Congress.
ISBN 0-306-81013-1

Original edition: Produced by Toby Byron/Multiprises

First Da Capo Press text edition, January 2001

The text of this book also appears in slightly different form in an illustrated edition by
the same author.

Text design by Jeff Williams
Set in 11-point Janson Text by Perseus Publishing Services

Published by Da Capo Press
A Member of the Perseus Books Group
http://www.dacapopress.com

3 4 5 6 7 8 9 — 04 03 02

Responding in 1949 to a "Blindfold Test" in which he was asked to rate unidentified records with one to five stars, Louis Armstrong said:

"I couldn't give anything less than two stars. You want to know why? Well, there's a story about the sisters who were talking about the pastor, and only one sister could appreciate the pastor. She said, 'If he's good, I can look through him and see Jesus. If he's bad, I can look over him and see Jesus.' That's the way I feel about music."

∼

I loved and respected Louis Armstrong. He was born poor, died rich, and never hurt anyone on the way.

— *Duke Ellington*

∼

The Abbot gazed at the boy who stood before him. He had intended to scold him, but as he looked at him, his expression sweetened. "Why did you stop, my child?" he asked. "You abandoned the vision in the middle. One mustn't do that. He's a prophet, and prophets must be revered."

— *Nikos Kazantzakis*

Contents

A Note to the New Edition   *xi*

Preface   *xv*

Part I
The Entertainer as Artist

One   *3*

Two   *13*

Three   *21*

Four   *41*

Five   *45*

Six   *59*

Seven   *73*

Contents

Part 2
The Artist as Entertainer

One   81

Two   91

Three   105

Four   117

Five   123

Six   133

Seven   145

Appendix: New Orleans   151

Discography   161

Bibliography   175

Acknowledgments   181

Index   185

A Note to the
New Edition

When the original edition of this book appeared in 1988, the argument I made in defense of Louis Armstrong's achievement as an entertainer was controversial. At that time, the idea that Armstrong's genius peaked and virtually ended with his 1920s records (the Hot 5s and Hot 7s) was fairly widespread, as was the hapless if not embarrassed critical response to his flair for comedy and devotion to his audience. Times change, and nothing gratifies me more than the realization that if I were writing this book today, I could take a lot of my old position for granted, and move on.

An illuminating study could be made of Armstrong criticism during his life and after. I remember when Dan Morgenstern was a lonely voice, obliged to defend not only Armstrong's later work, but the 1930s big band masterworks that are now routinely hailed as classics. The perspective keeps changing. Today, young listeners, who know nothing of the old battles, are more inclined to accept Armstrong whole, and are often surprised that battles were ever waged. His singing of pop songs is now experienced as an essential part of his achievement, to a degree that was not true even during the years when his vocal records ranked high on the charts. Or was it *because* they were so popular that critics dismissed them as secondary diversions?

I chose the Kazantzakis epigram (from *The Last Temptation of Christ*) to make the point that Louis Armstrong was a prophet and that to be completely understood and appreciated, his vision ought to be pursued to its end. Not everything he recorded is wonderful; like Homer, Armstrong nodded. Most of his legacy, however, is quite wonderful, and the delights will be found throughout the trajectory of his career. His genius can be relished in "Hello, Dolly!" as well as in "West End Blues." But there I go again, making an argument I just said no longer needed to be made. In truth, I continue to find myself going deeper into the vision.

For example, when Armstrong's 1966 recording of "Mame" was first released, I thought of it as amiable pop fluff, an obvious attempt to cash in on the "Hello, Dolly!" phenomenon, only without a trumpet solo. Having rediscovered it a couple of years ago, I now treasure it as a singular example of his alchemical powers and outsize musical personality. The song is so undistinguished one can scarcely imagine another singer attempting it. Yet Armstrong transforms it into something rich, expressive, exultantly swinging—can anyone be unmoved by the rapturous, room-filling, trombonelike melisma he consistently applies to the title name? Bing Crosby once asked, "Do you realize that the greatest pop singer in the world that ever was and ever will be forever and ever is Louis Armstrong?" He explained: "It's so simple. When he sings a sad song you feel like crying, when he sings a happy song you feel like laughing. What the hell else is there with pop singing?"

This book, like most books and articles about him, attempts to define Armstrong's influence, place, and historical stature. Yet at some point, that approach must give way to sheer pleasure, to a critical evaluation that takes the music on its own. We love Bach for Bach, not for his historical role in the development of Western culture. I think of Armstrong as America's Bach not because of his analogous place in the development of American culture, but because he imparts a similar joy, love, and ecstasy—the godly intimation that the world is much greater than we can ever imagine except through the visions of those geniuses, those prophets, who see farther than we can and proclaim the truth with the certainty of their art.

—*G. G.*
October 2000

Preface

Some books and articles call him Daniel Louis Armstrong. No one seems to know where the Daniel came from. Armstrong said it was not part of his name, and his baptismal certificate backs him up. You can start a fight over how he was addressed by friends. The Louis faction ("Hello, Dolly, this is Louissss, Dolly," the man sang) can get downright rude about those who pronounce it Louie. He wasn't French, they point out. But many friends and at least two wives called him both. The safest and by far the most common form of address was Pops, which is how he addressed everyone else—though in letters he would refer to male friends as "my boy" and to himself as "your boy." As a kid with a large trumpet player's mouth, he earned many nicknames, including Dippermouth or Dip, Gatemouth or Gate, and Satchelmouth or Satch. The last, unwittingly corrupted by a British journalist (Percy Brooks), survived as Satchmo. Insiders will tell you that no one ever called him that. No one but the man himself, who loved the name, and a hundred million fans who loved him.

xvi Preface

Through much of *Satchmo*, Louis Armstrong speaks in his
own voice in previously unpublished words.

Of Armstrong's many accomplishments, the least recognized
is his prolificacy as a writer of autobiographical prose. He was
by far the most expansive musician-writer jazz has ever known:
In addition to the famous memoir of his youth and an earlier
book so heavily ghosted as to be spurious, he wrote more than
two dozen magazine pieces, ranging from "Why I Like Dark
Women" for *Ebony* to a monthly column on jive talk for the
Harlem Tattler to a travel piece for *Holiday* to a review of Alan
Lomax's *Mr. Jelly Roll* for the *New York Times Book Review*. Yet
most of his writing was not intended for public scrutiny during
his lifetime. In addition to hundreds of chatty letters, he wrote
hundreds of pages of an autobiography intended for posthu-
mous publication. He was unschooled in spelling and gram-
mar, but he had an ear for language and could express himself
with enviable clarity in trim, speechlike cadences. Tallulah
Bankhead wrote in 1952, "He uses words like he strings notes
together—artistically and vividly." She was referring to his
conversation, which was peppered with an inventive brand of
slang, but the observation holds for his prose as well. Usually,
he typed single-space and fast. Sometimes he would write
dozens of pages at a clip in an always legible and authoritative
hand. He favored yellow typing paper and pens with green ink.

One might have thought that the letters incorporated in Max
Jones's and John Chilton's *Louis* (1971) would create interest in
a whole volume of them. But it was too soon; thirty years later,
such a compilation is reportedly underway. Armstrong was
adored throughout the world, yet his unself-conscious candor
made many people uncomfortable. His joyful presence became
a mask that interviewers, especially American telechat hosts,

were wary of lifting. Journalists invariably refrained from asking tough or even interesting questions, in spite of—or because of—Armstrong's willingness to respond honestly. Protective friends and editors, suffering from the effects of a Victorian education that Armstrong never had, frequently purged and prettified his writing.

Of the two books published under his name, the first, *Swing That Music* (1936), in many ways a fascinating document, has the distinction of being the first volume by or about a jazz musician (unless you consider Paul Whiteman a jazz musician), but was so bleached by a zealous ghostwriter—probably Horace Gerlach, who contributed the Music Section—that it's unreliable as biography or history. It disappeared soon enough. The justly renowned 1954 memoir *Satchmo: My Life in New Orleans* (hereafter *My Life*) is—despite the editor's prissy if generally sensible tidying up of a rapidly composed yet coherent manuscript—largely faithful to Armstrong's typescript, including inadvertently misspelled names.

Still, *My Life* was intended as the first in a series (a second volume was announced at the time of publication); it was based on the first 120-plus pages of a longer text that Armstrong continued to work on for years. Armstrong's long-standing manager and closest professional associate, Joe Glaser, is said to have terminated the published account with Armstrong's arrival in Chicago in 1922, because at that point he began to recount his problems with the law, a consequence of his lifelong fondness for marijuana, and the mob, which attempted to control his career. Armstrong frequently spoke of the larger text. He told Dan Morgenstern that he was mincing no words and that publication would have to be delayed until after his death; he read to Jack Bradley and others an excerpt on his belief in the curative value of pot that Bradley says had everyone present doubled up with laughter. Yet thirty years after Armstrong's death, only the section about marijuana has been located and published. Neither Queens College, which acquired the Armstrong archive, nor the executors of his estate know the rest of the manuscript's whereabouts. A close friend of Lucille Armstrong's and an administrator of the estate, Phoebe Jacobs, suggests the widow may have destroyed it. In 1974, Mrs. Armstrong told me, "Louis gave his writings to Joe Glaser, and I never saw them again." She also said she and Glaser were unhappy about the way *My Life* was edited and that "the second part" had been left out.

Other manuscripts, however, did turn up and were first published in the original (1988) edition of this book. In addition to numerous letters, some of them several pages long, they include the typescript for *My Life* (working title: *The Armstrong Story*), and two series of documents separated by more than twenty-five years. The first is a group of notebooks, written in 1944 for the Belgian writer Robert Goffin, who published a biography of Armstrong three years later but made little use of the material Armstrong sent him. Goffin's book is rough going, with its heavy dose of platitudinous politics, made-up dialogue ("Dey gwine down tuh Congo Place"), and countless misstatements, yet it relates facts about Armstrong's childhood that, though ignored by subsequent biographers, are confirmed by Armstrong's writings and my own research. When Goffin died, the notebooks were acquired by the Institute of Jazz Studies at Rutgers University.

The second manuscript, found among his papers, is far more remarkable. It consists of 129 pages written in longhand between 1968 and 1971 and falls into six sections. The most revealing is also the most troubling: a fifty-three-page memoir entitled "Negroe Neighborhood," in which Armstrong rails against the New Orleans blacks who failed, in his opinion, to stick together to improve their lot, and sings the praises of a Jewish family that gave him his first job at age seven, encouraged his singing, and enabled him to purchase his first cornet. Bitter, repetitive, achingly candid, and sometimes contradictory, it is an obsessive *cri du coeur*, unlike anything else he wrote. The second piece, a twenty-two-page open letter written after his second stay in the hospital, has the familiar ring of the irrepressible Satchmo. It tells of his conversion of all Beth Israel's nurses to his preferred physic, Swiss Kriss; his courtship of his wife Lucille; and his admiration for the great entertainer Bill Robinson. "New Orleans" amounts to a literary experiment: a forty-two-page dialogue that emerged as Armstrong copied a 1968 letter from someone he knew in the Colored Waif's Home, adding comments as the letter triggered them. It is a uniquely vivid montage of a vanished era and is published here in its entirety in the Appendix.

In addition, there are three short pieces—another attempt to retell the story of "Louis Armstrong and the Jewish Family in New Orleans, La. The Year of 1907"; "Barber Shops," a valentine to Corona, Queens; and an unfinished, deeply moving letter to all his fans, whom he feared he would never again see. For obvious reasons, I hesitated to use some of the controversial material. But not for long. Louis Armstrong was censored all his life by people who thought they knew his mind better than he did. They censored his books, attempted to gag him when he took one of the bravest stands on civil rights of any black entertainer in the 1950s, banned one of his records, and possibly destroyed or suppressed his autobiography. "To be great," Emerson said, "is to be misunderstood." Armstrong was misunderstood throughout his career. The more we know of him, the better we can reckon the man and his greatness.

Note: The Armstrong passages from previously unpublished sources are designated *Archive* (the 1968–71 material), *Goffin* (the 1944 notebooks), and *My* (the typescript for *Satchmo: My Life in New Orleans*). When typing, Armstrong liked to punctuate sentences with three or four periods (the old Walter Winchell style); I've removed them because they were likely to get confused with my own use of ellipses. The only editing I've done is the minimal kind any writer expects as courtesy—chiefly spelling and punctuation. Armstrong, who traveled with a well-thumbed dictionary, did not consider misspelled words "colorful."

Satchmo

Part One

THE ENTERTAINER AS ARTIST

One

GENIUS IS THE TRANSFIGURING AGENT. Nothing else can explain Louis Armstrong's ascendancy. He had no formal training, yet he alchemized the cabaret music of an outcast minority into an art that has expanded in ever-widening orbits for seventy-five years, with no sign of collapse. He played trumpet against the rules, and so new rules were written to acknowledge his standards. His voice was so harsh and grating that even black bandleaders were at first loath to let him use it, yet he became one of the most beloved and influential singers of all time. He was born with dark skin in a country where dark-skinned people were considered less than human and, with an ineffable radiance that transcends the power of art, forced millions of whites to reconsider their values. He came from "the bottom of the well, one step from hell," as one observer put it, but he died a millionaire in a modest home among working-class people. He was a jazz artist and a pop star who succeeded in theater and on records, in movies and on television. Yet until he died, he traveled in an unheated bus, playing one-nighters throughout the country, zigzagging around the world, demanding his due but never asking for special favors. He was an easy touch and is thought to have handed out hundreds of thousands of dollars to countless people down on their luck. Powerful persons, including royalty and the Pope, forgave him a measure of irreverence that would have been unthinkable coming from anyone else. Admirers describe him as a philosopher, a wise man, someone who knew all the secrets of how to live.

But few people knew him well, and many of those who were most possessive about his art were offended by his popularity. The standard line about Armstrong during his lifetime, rendered in James Lincoln Collier's 1983 biography, goes like this: Louis Armstrong was a superb artist in his early years, *the* exemplar of jazz improvisation, until fame forced him to compromise, at which point he became an entertainer, repeating himself and indulging a taste for low humor. In his 1981 Armstrong discography, Hans Westerberg notes that he "was generally despised by critics and jazz purists during the last decades of his career." *Despised!*—the word sounds jarring, overbaked. Louis Armstrong despised? Yet, in fact, he was beset by damning reviews for nearly forty years. He was excoriated for playing pop tunes, fronting a swing band, appearing with media stars, sticking to a standardized repertory, engaging in vaudeville routines, making scatological jokes, mugging, entertaining. When he knocked the Beatles from their number 1 perch in 1964 with "Hello, Dolly!", the last record by a jazz musician or (excepting

Frank Sinatra) a prerock artist ever to top the charts, the jazz community was ambivalent.

Seventeen years after his death, he made the charts again, with a song cut in 1967, "What a Wonderful World"—the only track from the movie *Good Morning, Vietnam* to get a new life. According to statistician Joel Whitburn, who uses ratio and sales figures to simulate pop charts going back to the 1890s, Armstrong's first "hit" was "Muskrat Ramble": number 8 in 1926. No other singer comes close to spanning sixty-two years on the charts. One can't imagine a single contemporary of Armstrong's in the 1920s—Al Jolson? Ethel Waters? Bing Crosby?—enjoying the same degree of success six decades later. Armstrong's undying popularity is as significant a tribute to the timelessness of his music as is the undiminished purity of such epochal masterworks as "West End Blues" or "Potato Head Blues." A jazz aesthetics incapable of embracing Louis Armstrong whole is unworthy of him, and of the American style of music-making that he, more than any other individual, engendered.

Armstrong was an artist who happened to be an entertainer, an entertainer who happened to be an artist—as much an original in one role as the other. He revolutionized music, but he also revolutionized expectations about what a performer could be. In the beginning, he was an inevitable spur for the ongoing American debate between high art and low. As his genius was accepted in classical circles around the world, a microcosm of the dispute took root in the jazz community, centered on his own behavior. Elitists who admired the musician capable of improvising solos of immortal splendor were embarrassed by the comic stage ham. One reason, surely, is that critics were frustrated (far more than Armstrong ever was) by the fact that relatively few of his fans knew just how profound his stature was. How many of those who joined Benny Goodman's swing caravan in the thirties or rocked to Chuck Berry in the fifties or savored the increased vibrato that became fashionable in the brass sections of symphony orchestras knew the extent to which they were living in a world created by the famous gravel-mouthed clown? How many appreciated what Miles Davis meant when he said, "You know you can't play anything on the horn that Louis hasn't played—I mean even modern," or Bing Crosby, when he called Armstrong "the beginning and the end of music in America," or Virgil Thompson, when he wrote that his "improvisation would seem to have combined the highest reaches of instrumental virtuosity with the most tensely disciplined melodic structure and the most sponta-neous emotional expression, all of which in one man you must admit is pretty rare"?

Perhaps because it elicits concentrated emotional and car-nal responses, music often makes us pietists and hypocrites. Having experienced great music, we are torn between pro-mulgating it and protecting it from the great unwashed. Armstrong would have none of that, and his career superbly demonstrates the democratization of an art conceived, as he insisted, "in the cause of happiness." He is the only major figure in Western culture who influenced the music of his time equally as an instrumentalist and singer. His popularity enabled him to shatter countless racial obstacles, while his manner undermined Europhile assumptions about the way an artist was supposed to present himself. He advocated and perfected purity of tone and obeisance to melody; patented the rhythmic gait known as swing; transformed a polyphonic folk music into a soloist's art; established the expressive weight of blues tonality; proved the durability of harmonic improvisation. But he also relished the tradition of humor that had grown out of the black archetype in minstrel shows and had become a mainstay of black entertainment throughout the first two decades of his life. In 1938, he paid tribute to such monologists as Bert Williams (whose records he collected and whom he had begun to parody on stage as early as 1924) with his Elder Eatmore sermons.

Constance Rourke observed in *American Humor* that two of the three primary nineteenth-century American theatrical archetypes—those of the Yankee and backwoodsman—were shy of emotion, indulging at best in "mock melancholy." In the third, minstrelsy, "emotion was near the surface, surging obscurely through the choruses and walkarounds, but this was always communal, never individual . . . individual emotion was sponged out." This despite the "strong individualism" of actors who subverted minstrelsy's ritualism. Yet she also noted that while Negro humor shared with the other archetypes a sense of "comic triumph," it remained unique on two counts: It developed "conscious" satire, and it recognized the absurd, which Rourke described as "an unreasonable headlong triumph launching into the realm of the preposterous."

To separate Armstrong the sublime trumpeter from Armstrong the irrepressible stage wag not only curbs a magnanimous artist to satisfy a misguided appeal to Kulchur, but underestimates the absurdist humor that informs his serious side. His ability to balance the emotional gravity of the artist with the communal good cheer of the entertainer helped enable him to demolish the Jim Crow/Zip Coon/Ol' Dan Tucker stereotypes. In their place he installed the liberated black man, the pop performer as world-renowned artist who dressed stylishly, lived high, slapped palms with the Pope, and regularly passed through whites-only portals, leaving the doors open behind him. Americans loved Armstrong, and he counted on that love to do what only the greatest artists are prepared to do—show the world to itself in a new light. By the late 1940s, fashions changed and many blacks and not a few whites took offense at his clowning, equating it with racial servility. But an Uncle Tom, though he may stoop to conquer, consciously demeans himself. Armstrong would have considered ludicrous an attempt to equate his style of entertainment with self-abasement. He was as much himself rolling his eyes and mugging as he was playing the trumpet. His fans understood that, but intellectuals found the whole effect too damn complicated.

Significantly, Armstrong disdained black entertainers who went along with the minstrel tradition, still rife in the 1920s, of using burnt cork. Which is one reason he so admired dancer Bill "Bojangles" Robinson:

> To me he was the greatest comedian + dancer in my race. He didn't need blackface to be funny. Better than Bert Williams. I personally Admired Bill Robinson because he was immaculately dressed—you could see the quality of his clothes even from the stage. Stopped every show. He did

not wear old raggedy top hat and tails with the pants cut
off, black cork with thick white lips, etc. But the audiences
loved him very much. He was funny from the first time
he opened his mouth till he finished. So to me that's what
counted, his material is what counted. (*Archive*)

Armstrong loved sharing the stage with Robinson and
mourned the fact that there could never be another like him.
He'd have hated the idea, but his success was one reason
Robinson's style soon appeared antiquated. The thing that
Louis put onstage with unequivocal self-confidence, border-
ing on macho arrogance, was a personal magnetism that
transcended every trace of racial inferiority. You can see it in
his earliest film appearances. In 1932 he made a short called
Rhapsody in Black and Blue, in which a hen-pecked husband
falls asleep and dreams he's king in a heaven in which Armstrong performs at his command. The husband is the stereo-
typical lazy black, stereotypically performed and guaranteed
to make a modern audience squirm. That's nothing compared to what Armstrong is asked to embody. The whole
deck is stacked against him. First, he's garbed in a leopard
skin; second, he's ankle deep in soap bubbles; third, he performs "You Rascal You" and "Shine" ("I take troubles all
with a smile . . . that's why they call me Shine"). None of it
holds him back. He transcends the racist trappings by his in-
difference to every sling and arrow. The director/writer is
trying to tell the audience one thing. Armstrong is telling it
something entirely different—he's doing it not only with the
magnificence of his music, but with his physical muscularity,
his carriage, his boding sexuality, the look in his eye. Blacks

understood this in the 1930s and made him a national hero. When styles changed and black audiences abandoned him, Armstrong was wounded and he never got over it. In 1969, in a moment of uncharacteristic self-pity, he complained of being called "a white folks' nigger" and retorted, "Believe it. The white folks did everything that's decent for me. . . . They never let us down with their attendance and their appreciation."

On every level of his art/entertainment, Armstrong combined musical inspiration with a beguiling knowledge of the anomalous. The result is manifested in obvious ways: in his use of nonsense syllables—scat singing—to replace or supplement the lyrics of a song or to facilitate vocal improvisation; in song titles that celebrate sex or pot or food, usually in slang too inside even for most musicians; in the humor that deflates the sentimental pretensions of pop songs; in the stage routines that persistently undermine the seriousness of his own art, so that vainglorious brilliance is balanced by an indecorous wit that establishes casual mutuality with the audience. Yet his familiarity with the absurd runs deeper still, producing the fundamental detachment or irony that allowed him to transfigure the music of his day.

When Armstrong came on the scene, an entertainer would look at lead sheets and choose the songs he liked or felt were right for his style. Blacks quickly realized that song-pluggers and producers were not going to offer them the best material and learned to make do by creating their own or by transforming the chaff. As in so many other areas, Armstrong led the way. At first he played the so-called traditional repertory, a portfolio of originals to which he contributed many classics, including "I Wish I Could Shimmy Like My Sister Kate" (which he sold for fifty dollars), "Muskrat Ramble" (which he allowed Kid Ory to claim), "Struttin' with Some Barbecue" (one of several pieces he allowed his second wife, pianist Lil Hardin, to claim), "Weather Bird," "Wild Man Blues," "Cornet Chop Suey," "Don't Forget to Mess Around," and more. Then he began recording pop songs, good and bad: lovely ballads, trite novelties, Cuban and Hawaiian songs, and anything else the traffic would allow. He took it all, having known apparently from the beginning that no song could diminish him and that he could lift most songs far beyond their earthly calling. Though he appreciated quality—he quickly established himself as a loyal and matchless interpreter of Fats Waller and Hoagy Carmichael—he was undaunted by junk.

Armstrong personified a strangely new idea in music, one that became axiomatic when Trummy Young outlined it in a song: "'Taint What You Do, It's the Way That You Do It." At his best, Heifetz is as good as his material. Armstrong stands above his. This phenomenon would seem to posit a colossal musical ego, able to digest all songs in the spirit of noblesse oblige. Except that it won't work unless the performer is willing to get into the dirt with his material and have fun with it.

When Armstrong takes a first-class song like "Stardust," he discards everything a conventional performer would seize. Using mild embellishment and bold improvisation, he rephrases, restates, amplifies, and finally re-creates the melody. He is equally unintimidated by the lyric, which he turns into a pastiche of words and moans. That song, which most performers find difficult to sing straight, is in Armstrong's hands the starting post for an emotional statement far more potent than the original. He is no less compelling on a relatively trite piece, for example "Lazy River," in which he interrupts the record to observe, "Boy, am I riffin' tonight," then makes good his promise with a mind-bending glissando that still has trumpet players shaking their heads in wonder. Nowhere is his irony more breathtaking than in "Laughin' Louie," in which he discards the rum tune after a few measures, addresses the other musicians in the role of a laughing buffoon, and then plays an unaccompanied melody—recalled, he says, from his youth—of immutably stark and haunting beauty. What manner of man is this Laughin' Louie who can play music to make the angels weep?

Two

IN DISTINGUISHING BETWEEN the artist/entertainer that was young Armstrong and the entertainer/artist he became, you have to take into account the changing identity of his audience. His earliest audiences, in New Orleans and Chicago, were made up of fellow performers and fans drawn from insular communities that evolved with the new music. In those days, when he was shy and somewhat apprehensive about striking out on his own, Armstrong proved himself by pleasing his colleagues. After tearing his lips apart with high-note displays of virtuosity, he came to realize—with the help of a powerful manager—that there was a much larger audience that expected more and less of him: more personality, less grandstanding. He eventually grew relatively indifferent to the musicians onstage with him. He took no part in hiring or firing band members, expecting them to back him up in a creative and professional manner. He had turned his focus to the other side of the footlights, though—like all real artists—he continued to satisfy himself first.

Armstrong knew the difference between a comic duet with his foil Velma Middleton and a perfect rueful chorus of "Black and Blue," which he was likely to do at the same concert. He also knew that a thin line separated the two, since the abiding job was to please the audience, a mandate he took very seriously. Like Shakespeare, he wasn't so much ahead of his time as he was plugged directly into it. For two hundred years, idiot scholars with a class problem have tried to prove that Shakespeare couldn't have written his plays because he wasn't well educated or politically connected. Perhaps if Armstrong's genius were preserved only in scores and on records, some future scholar might try to prove that the man who virtually invented jazz and swing, who put blues improvisation and the vernacular voice on the map, could not have been an untutored black kid from Jane Alley. It must have been somebody trained in the subtleties of phrasing, intonation, and harmony. Picture the headline in the *Times:* Professor Emmeff Offers New Armstrong Theory, says there were two men, the first died mysteriously in the early 1930s, was replaced by an impostor hired by a venal manager to fulfill fifty years of signed contracts.

Yet what made Armstrong an innovative entertainer was his ability to show how the same impulses and techniques that went into the early masterpieces could become the lingua franca for a music of universal appeal. The artist, however, always governed the key musical choices: what notes to play and how to play them. An indefatigable propagandist for playing straight melody and seductive rhythms, he was never so hidebound by fashion or his success that he stopped developing. If the later Armstrong was incapable of the complex rhythmic bravura of the 1927 "Hotter Than That," the devilish imp of the twenties could not have produced the resplendent mid-register lyricism of the 1955 "Blue Turning Gray Over You." Armstrong never declared himself an artist or an entertainer. But in 1932, when applying for a passport, he gave his occupation as "actor and musician." Although he had appeared in two or three short films by that time, he had not yet done any acting per se. He undoubtedly used the term in the same generic sense that every vaudevillian, minstrel, and cabaret performer of the day did. Music was his art, as dancing was Fred Astaire's and joking was Jack Benny's. They were all actors. From the time he sang for pennies in a boys' vocal quartet in the streets of New Orleans, Armstrong was a showman as well as a musician.

Which is not to say he didn't know who he was. He seems to have known what he could do long before he did it, and he carried himself with the dignity and assurance of a man fully aware of the magnitude of his accomplishment. He knew he was the best, knew he was the only genuine king of swing, knew it and (when a young gunslinger or an overpromoted white celebrity musician forced his hand) proved it—not with talk, but with his trumpet. But unlike those critics who would have had him play chamber jazz for aficionados all his life, he recognized the obligation of a gift that could bring his music far beyond its original coterie. The caveat that held "My Bucket's Got a Hole in It" to be better jazz material than "Body and Soul" because it embodied old (read: folk) traditions never impressed him. Yet he remained steadfast in his devotion to the principles he learned in New

Orleans and defended them with controversial fervor in the bop years.

In a 1948 discussion in which Barney Bigard said, "You got to move along with the times," Armstrong replied: "I'm doing something different all the time, but I always think of them fine old cats way down in New Orleans—Joe and Bunk and Tio and Buddy Bolden—and when I play my music, that's what I'm listening to. The way they phrased so pretty and always on the melody, and none of that out-of-the-world music, that pipedream music, that whole modern malice." That statement, with its unconscious echo of Charles Lamb's "the measured malice of music," was widely quoted by the modernists as proof that Armstrong had fallen into a rut. They missed the irony as well as the poignancy of his plea. Here was ol' Satchmo declaring solidarity with a tradition that had virtually excommunicated him fifteen years earlier for going modern. Targeted from both sides, Armstrong sometimes bellowed back. Usually, he kept his own counsel and looked straight ahead—at the audience.

If Armstrong was as accepting, generous, and loving as his friends, acquaintances, and musicians claim (no man personified better the credo *Homo sum, et humani nihil a me alienum est*), he was also proud and competitive, sometimes fiercely so, easily miffed when another musician foxed him onstage. Everyone in his life, including four wives, knew that the trumpet came first. He lived life as he pleased, which meant constant work and lots of play. He was a sensualist who smoked pot daily, devoured rich, simple foods (he often signed his letters "Red beans and ricely yours"), drank heartily (he liked bourbon and slivovitz, a plum brandy), and enjoyed the company of countless women. Still, he always hit the gig on time and played to the peak of his amazing energy. The attorney Charles L. Black, Jr., a white Texan who was part of the team that litigated *Brown v. Board of Education*, has traced his journey from "good old boy" Austin to the Supreme Court to an encounter with Armstrong's music at a whites-only hotel in 1931. He wrote of that evening: "Louis seemed—as was guessed, I believe, of Paganini—under demonic possession—strengthened and guided by a Daemon. [He] played mostly with his eyes closed; just before he closed them they seemed to have ceased to look outward, to have turned inward, to the world out of which the music was to flow."

In the course of talking to dozens of people who knew and worked with Pops or simply heard him and were changed forever, I came across two ideas repeatedly. The first was this: What you saw was what you got—he was every bit as bighearted and open and genuine as he seemed onstage. The second, relating to the later years, referred to a transforming magic that occurred right before he walked into the spotlight. I was lucky enough to experience it firsthand. In 1968, as an undergraduate in charge of college concerts, I arranged for Armstrong to play at a convocation at Grinnell College in Iowa. He never knew about two incidents that marred the occasion for me and seem now to delineate the bastard place jazz occupies in America's cultural life: Nearly two dozen intellectuals and artists were on campus to participate in a series of discussions and to receive honorary degrees, yet the college refused to award one to Armstrong; outside the gymnasium where he performed, a handful of students picketed because they wanted a rock group.

The band arrived and repaired to the gym locker room to dress. I had never seen Armstrong before and was determined to shake his hand. I chatted with his pianist, Marty Napoleon, who told me Pops was isolated in the back with his doctor but would be happy to see me before they went on. He talked about how great he was and what an honor it was to travel with him—you'd have thought they'd just started together, but Napoleon had already been on the road with him two years. (He talks the same way about Louis today.) Suddenly, there he was, an old man in a loose tuxedo, his brown coloring tinctured with gray, his eyes slightly rheumy, the scar on his upper lip (which had been rebuilt with grafts a decade before) alarmingly raw. Doc, a congenial white-haired man, walked him to a bench, and he sat there looking downcast. Napoleon introduced me to Doc (Dr. Alexander Schiff), who brought me over to the bench and said, "Pops, this is Gary Giddins. He produced the gig and would like very much to meet you." He put out his hand and stood, his eyes brightening and his smile rising like the sun. "Hello, Pops," he said. A jolt ran through my arm, though his grasp was slack. I mumbled something, wanting to embrace him and tell him how much his music meant to me, but was restrained by how fatigued and fragile he looked. He peered out at the gym, and I thought: This is just another one-nighter . . . in Iowa. Why does he still bother?

A few seconds later he said he was ready, and I walked out front to watch the show. Between the locker room and the steps leading up to the stage was the space of a few feet cast in shadow by stark lighting. Each musician disappeared into it before attaining the stage. As Armstrong emerged into the light, arms slightly raised, palms out, he appeared transfigured. The ashen color was gone, the eyes blazed, the smile blinded. When he sang, he engaged the crowd eyeball to eyeball. When he blew trumpet, he kept his eyes open, but the pupils rolled upward as though he were no longer in the room. His huge tone was as golden and unspotted as ever. Each musician had a feature number, at which time Armstrong walked into the shadows to rest. He would return glowing with energy.

I've often thought that had I been a critic then, I might have disdained the same old same old: the inevitable "Indiana" opener, the excessive drum solo, the obligatory female singer, "Hello, Dolly!" But maybe not. The set worked. And when Armstrong was onstage, nothing else mattered. He carried the weight of his own myth in all its grandeur, but it was the myth made human—made possible.

Three

HOW BETTER TO START AN AMERICAN MYTH than with a flag-waving birthday: July 4, 1900. The man who established America's preeminence in the world of twentieth-century music is ushered in amid roman candles and a couple of killings in the first year of the new age—or so he told us. But it isn't true. The alleged date of Louis Armstrong's birth, like that of the Battle of Hastings, is a bit of information that everyone seems to know. Armstrong himself was steadfast about it, even filling in details of the Independence Day action he said he learned from his mother. Many scholars doubted him, figuring the year was correct but the month and day were chosen later—impoverished blacks in that era often chose July 4 when they didn't know the actual day. After all, Louis enjoyed no annual birthday celebrations as a child. In his 1983 biography *Louis Armstrong: An American Genius*, Collier wrote, "There is not a single document to prove that Armstrong even existed until he was eighteen years old," and then adduced a birthdate of 1898, on the

grounds that a couple of contemporaries thought he was
older and because a 1918 draft form shows the registrar
started to write July 4, 18—, then crossed out the 8 and wrote
1900. Collier assumes that Armstrong shaved two years to
avoid the draft during World War I, which makes no sense.
The Selective Service Act of 1917 drafted men between the
ages of twenty-one and thirty; when it was amended in September 1918, at which time Armstrong registered, the age
was lowered to eighteen. Armstrong made himself no less
vulnerable by declaring himself eighteen than twenty. In any
case, there *are* earlier documents, and they show that he al-
tered his age for the same reason most adolescents do—to
appear older, not younger.

Louis Armstrong was born August 4, 1901, in a ram-
shackle house on a squalid block-long lane in New Orleans
called Jane Alley, between Perdido and Poydras streets. His
mother, either fifteen or sixteen years old at the time, was
Mary Albert, who had come to the city from the sugarcane
fields of Boutte, Louisiana; his father, who abandoned
them shortly after his son's birth, was William Armstrong,
whose family may have come from St. Charles Parish. On
August 25, three weeks after he was born, Louis was taken
to the white Sacred Heart of Jesus Church, on Lopez
Street, to be baptized. He wrote that his father's mother,
Josephine, a Catholic who raised him during his first four
or five years, took him to church that day, but it was probably a white neighbor named Catherine Walker, who
cosponsored him with the Reverend J. M. Toohey. Since
his mother, to whom he returned to live at age five, was

Baptist, it's unlikely he ever worshiped in a Roman Catholic church again. The baptismal register certifies his birthday and the names of his parents. Additional confirmation of his age is found in the 1910 census record for the 1300 block of Perdido Street, which lists a family of three at a rooming house at 1303 Perdido: Thomas Lee, the twenty-four-year-old "head" of the house, who gave his occupation as laborer on a schooner (Louis mentions him as one of several "stepfathers" in *My Life*); Mary Albert, his twenty-five-year-old "companion," who gave her occupation as laundress; and Louis Armstrong, her eight-year-old son. The census was taken April 22 or 23, 1910, so Louis would have been nine in August.

Why did he make himself out to be older? In 1918, Louis's career as a musician was beginning to take off. Kid Ory invited him to replace King Oliver in his band, and Fate Marable wanted to recruit him for an orchestra that made interstate tours on a Mississippi steamer. A year earlier, the United States Navy had shut down Storyville, the notorious red-light district of New Orleans, and it's likely that officials were cracking down on the remaining dives. Cabaret owners may have had doubts about hiring a minor, and even if things remained loose in New Orleans, the same might not be true of places like Davenport, where the steamboat docked. Perhaps the responsible Marable asked him to get proof of age. It was also in 1918 that Louis married the young prostitute Daisy. The one place a black seventeen-year-old could get "proof" he was eighteen was the local draft board. Armstrong wrote:

Early 1918 came in. And with the flu sickness kind of letting
up, and the United States finally getting after the Kaiser
and his boys in fine fashion, and the last draft call [con-
scripting] 18 to 45 years olds, which fit me just right, I went
on down to the draft board and registered. I sure was a
proud fellow when I could feel back there in my hip pocket
and feel my draft card, expecting to go to war any minute
and fight for Uncle Sam. Or, *Blow* for him. (*My*)

Collier doesn't believe Armstrong really wanted to fight,
and neither do I. He avoided physical violence all his life, as
well as anything that would keep him from his music.
Moreover, he admits in *My Life* that he took a job he de-
tested, driving a coal cart from 7 A.M. to 5 P.M., to ensure a
deferment. He most likely left the draft post feeling
"proud" because he had proof in his pocket that he was a
man, and could play nights at Henry Matranga's honky-
tonk on Perdido Street. Perhaps he chose July 4 for its patriotic ring, or because it was customary for boys who didn't
know their birthdate to use it, or because he had more than
an intimation—this is confirmed by several musicians who
knew him in 1918—of his future greatness and had the wit
to pick a date that everyone would remember. Even so, for a
man to walk into a draft board at seventeen and declare
himself of age, he must have been exceedingly confident the
army wouldn't call him. Either that or he actually considered joining up—perhaps to "Blow" with a military band.
(Word must have reached New Orleans about the black
369th Infantry Regiment Band, led by Lt. James Reese Europe.) As for the clerk mistakenly writing the date 18—,

he'd have gotten used to writing it; most of the new draftees were nineteen or twenty.

The new birthdate stuck. It served him well in Chicago, when he went to work with King Oliver at the Lincoln Gardens in 1922, showing he was over twenty-one. When Joe Glaser took over his career, he recognized it as a press agent's dream and burned it into the public mind. Armstrong himself was utterly attached to the date—he clings to it in all his personal papers, even his photo albums, in which snapshots are captioned, e.g., "This was 1937, when I was 37 years old." When Armstrong wrote *My Life*, he insisted that the street where he was born was James Alley, not Jane Alley, "as some people call it." He didn't live there long and that's how he remembered it. In later years, jazz historians showed him he was wrong. When he sketched his youth in 1969 in a memoir titled "Negroe Neighborhood," he wrote *Jane Alley* in block capitals twice, but he held firm to his famous birthdate. The memoir begins with a solitary third-person reference, possibly to certify his true name (no Daniel). He refers to his mother, here and elsewhere, alternately as Mary Ann and Mayann:

> Louis Armstrong was born July 4th 1900, in the Back
> O' Town JANE ALLEY section in New Orleans. Mary Ann
> [was] the mother of two children who she raised and
> supported all by herself. We did not have a father. They
> must have separated soon after we were born. Mama Lucy
> (my sister) nor I can recall seeing him. Anyway Mayann,
> that's what everybody called her, worked hard to see that we
> had food and a place to sleep. We moved from Back O'

Town JANE ALLEY into the Third Ward (into the city),
located at Franklyn and Perdido Streets, where the Honky
Tonks were located. A row of Negroes of all characters were
living in rooms which they rented and fixed up the best
way they could. We were *All* poor. The privies (the toilets)
were put into a big yard, one side for the men and one side
for the women . . . The folks, young and old, would go
out into the yard and sit or lay around, or the old folks
would sit in their rockin' chairs, etc. out in the sun until it
was outhouse time . . . Everything went on in the yard. I
remember one moonlit night a woman hollared out into the
yard to her daughter—she said (real loud), "You, Marandy,
you'd better come into this house, laying out there with
nothing on top of you but that thin nigger." Marandy said,
"Yassum." (*Archive*)

Some say that Armstrong never had a childhood, others
that he never had anything else. All his life he worked hard
and played hard. The deprivation of his early years left its
mark: After he became an international celebrity, he would
astonish other musicians with his genuine gratitude for such
amenities as a limousine or posh hospitality. In all his published writings, he remains uncomplaining about those early
years. Here is a man who saw life from the gutter up
and learned to accept it all. Jane Alley was an area so ridden
with violence and vice it was known as the Battlefield. For
many of his friends, pimps and whores and gamblers and
razor-wielding badasses were role models. Armstrong, of
course, was different. In order to create music of the spheres
you have to be able to hear it, and Armstrong heard it as a

siren call leading him out of hell. One has to believe that the generosity-bordering-on-obsession with which he took his music to the masses reflected his own pragmatic confidence in its healing power. Raised in a house of cards in the middle of a gale, he credited music and his mother's love and wisdom with getting him through. He accepted with equanimity the possibility that Mayann, who left him in the care of his grandmother until he was five, may have worked as a prostitute:

> My mother went to live in another fast neighborhood, down
> on Liberty and Perdido (a cheap storyville section—what I
> mean by that is the prostitutes did not receive as much pay
> for their time as the whores did down in Storyville).
> Whether Maryann was selling fish (HUSTLING) I could
> not say. If she was, she certainly kept it out of sight. One
> thing, everybody from the church folks to the lowest gave
> her the greatest respect, and she was always glad to say hello
> to anybody, no matter who. Come what may, she figured.
> And with it all, she held her head up at all times. Nothing
> excited her. What she didn't have, she did without. She
> never envied no one, or anything they may have. I guess I
> inherited that part of life from Mayann. (*My*)

Mayann inherited part of her outlook from an upbringing in the country, an isolated Creole area about seventy miles west of New Orleans off Route 90. The riverfront is a strip about forty miles long, with vestigial plantation buildings and flat cane fields that were once patrolled by peacocks instead of dogs. Today the area is dominated largely by oil interests that have polluted the water and added carcinogenic horrors to the natural ones endured by a people situated between swamps and the river, and beset by floods and disease. In back of the riverfront part called Luling is Boutte (pronounced Bou-tee), a small community, which, in Mayann's time, was connected to the front by the vast sugarcane plantations. (The largest of these, ironically, was the Ellington Plantation, now the site of a Monsanto complex.) Every kind of Creole mix could be found there, and at the bottom of the heap were the "black blacks," like Mayann, who had the fewest opportunities and were generally the last to leave.

Boutte-born Eddie Edwards, who in 1983 created the Louis Armstrong Foundation in New Orleans to tutor gifted children, says, "Everyone dumped on the black blacks, even the blacks, and if you were black black you had no idea of what the white world was like. Mayann left with absolutely nothing, and the only alternative she had to being a field worker in the country was being a servant in the city. Arriving in Jane Alley meant she started out at the very bottom. Creoles were more educated, they had schools out here and could speak English and French, but the blacks in New Orleans were working-class. They had nothing but the live-and-let-live spirit of the country where your survival was imperiled every day by floods, disease, and worse."

How much time Armstrong himself spent in the country is not known. He didn't write about it or, more significantly, title songs after it. But he had a favorite story that he occasionally told his concert audiences, including one in Chicago in 1962:

I was telling about the time when I was a little bitty boy in my mother's hometown of Boutte, Louisiana. I was about five years old, cute little ol' thing, too. Mayann, my mother you know, she said to me one morning, "Son, run down to the pond and get a bucket of water for your mama." And I cut out for that water, and Mayann dug me when I come back without the water and pooooh, boy! She said, "Boy, where is that water?" I said, "Well, mama, there's a big old rusty alligator in that pond and I didn't get that water." She said, "Oh, boy, go get that water. Don't you know that alligator is scared of you as you are of him!" I told her, "Mama, if he's scared of me as I am of him, that water isn't fit to drink."

On another occasion, when he told the story at a record session, he prefaced it by saying that as a kid "we lived in a little town called Boutte, Louisiana." Some of the older residents can still recall Mayann's mother working in the fields, and some familial contact must have been maintained because Louis's sister would drive out at least as late as the 1960s. Edwards believes Boutte offered a lifeline that helped ensure Louis's independence in the corrupt city.

Mayann probably met Willie Armstrong in the city, and it was her cousin Issac Myles, a forty-three-year-old laborer living with his wife, Francis, and four children at 723 Jane (according to the census record of 1900), who found her a place to live; after June 1900, she moved next door to the Myles family, at 719, where Louis was born. When Louis turned five, he was returned to his mother's care. On that day, he encountered Jim Crow and jazz, and was confronted with the Dickensian responsibility of helping to care for his sick mother and baby sister, Beatrice (known since childhood as Mama Lucy), born two years after him during a brief reconciliation between Mayann and Willie.

The neighborhood woman who brought him back to Jane Alley on the streetcar scolded him when he obliviously sat in the white section. He asked her what the signs in the other area ("For Colored Patrons Only") said, and was told, "Boy, don't ask so many questions, sit down damnit!" (*My*) He recalled that it was at his first reunion with his mother that she advised him to take a physic every day, a habit that became an obsession and the subject of much of his earthy humor. In the 1969 memoir, he compared the "pure" food he ate in the home of Jewish neighbors with the tasty but "heavy" food at home ("I loved the way she used to cook those Cat Heads— P.S. bisquits and molasses. Dee-licious. Yea, make you lick your fingers"), and explained the need for homemade herbal laxatives:

> Their food was always pure—the best. I noticed whenever I ate with them I would even sleep better. Much different from the heavy foods Mayann, Mama Lucy, and me had to eat. I had the stomach ache all the time. Mama Lucy suffered with some kind of fits. One of those big names they called it. She damn near died. Mayann told Mama Lucy and me, since we have to eat this heavy kind of food because we couldn't do any better, too poor, we will just have to make the best of it. [She said] the food that you all eat today you must take a good purge and clean your little stomachs out

thoroughly. They will keep the germs away. We both gave
Mayann our word that we would stay physic-minded for the
rest of our lives. (*Archive*)

He attended school and church sporadically, ran errands,
sold rags and coal, cleaned graves for tips, sang on the street
in a vocal quartet for pennies. He also got into fights, and
into trouble with the law for hustling stolen newspapers and
discarded food. He claims he heard the legendary trumpeter
Buddy Bolden at the end of his career, in 1905 or 1906, playing in front of Funky Butt Hall (Kenna's Hall), near his
home. It should probably be pointed out that Armstrong's
neighborhood was nearly a mile west of Storyville. Number-
less writers have tended to place every Orleanian honky-tonk
and whore's crib in the much romanticized area set aside by
Alderman Story's ordinance of 1897. Armstrong occasionally
tried to correct the misconception but ultimately acceded to
the myth. Still, contrary to recent biographies, he never lived
in Storyville, which was shut down in 1917, and he almost
certainly never played there while the ordinance was in
effect. The honky-tonks he frequented (see Appendix)—
including Spano's, Savocca's, Ponce's, and Henry Matranga's,
where he got his first important job as a musician—were in
the area where he lived, near Perdido Street. "Gee, that
neighborhood had a lot to offer," he would later muse without a trace of sarcasm. He could, of course, be sarcastic as
hell about other aspects of the Old South:

The other white nationalities kept the Jewish people with
fear constantly. As far as us Negroes, well I don't have to ex-

plain anything. Am sure you already know. At ten years old I
could see the bluffings that those old fatbelly, stinking, very
smelly dirty white folks were putting down. It seems that
the only thing that they cared about was their shotguns,
those oldtime shotguns which they had strapped around
them. So they got full of their mint julip or that bad whiskey
the poor white trash were guzzling down like water, then
when they got so damn drunk they'd go out of their minds,
it's Nigger Hunting time. Any Nigger.

They wouldn't give up until they would find one. From
then on, Lord have mercy on the poor darkie. Then they
would torture the poor darkie, as innocent as he may be.
Then they would get their usual ignorant Cheshire Cat
laughs before they would shoot him down like a dog. My
my my, those were the days. (*Archive*)

My Life is not quite the we-were-poor-but-happy idyll
many people remember it as. Between the lines and sometimes in the lines are indications—albeit watered down,
compared with his unpublished writings—of violence and
misery, nightmare episodes exacerbated by his abiding resentment of the absentee Willie, and of other neighborhood
men who abandoned their responsibilities. Through it all,
he was brought up to be independent and to think for himself. "My mother had one thing . . . and that was good common sense and respect for human beings, yea. That's my
diploma. . . . I was taught to respect a man or woman until
they prove in my estimation that they don't deserve it."
Mayann and Uncle Ike Myles were so determined not to let

him wallow in self-pity that they even described slavery as just another obstacle to be overcome:

> Mayann and Uncle Ike had a little touch of slavery, because their relatives before them came up right in it. They said the slaves acted dumb and ignorant, kept malice and hate among themselves so the whites took advantage of it—especially when they were full of their mint julips. They couldn't keep a secret among themselves. They would make plans among themselves and one Negro would double cross them by sneaking back and tell the white man everything they had planned to do. Quite naturally they would make him the head nigger. At least for the time being anyway . . . Slavery was just like anything else. B.S. (*Archive*)

The extent to which his double education—brutish in the streets, fortifying at home—colored his observations of the adult world is apparent throughout the frequently acrimonious memoir of 1969, written during an apparent bout of depression brought on by his stay in the hospital. At times Armstrong sputters with rage:

> We never did try to get together and show the younger Negroes such as myself to try . . . with just a little encouragement I could really have done something worthwhile. But instead we did nothing but let the young upstarts know that they were young and simple and that was that. Never a warm word for doing anything important came to their minds. My nationality (Negroes) took advantage of my

mother because . . . Mayann gave birth to Mama Lucy and
me. She had to struggle with us until we grew up. After
grabbing a little schooling and a job at a very young age, I
myself will never forget. I will try to forgive. They were in
an alley or on the streetcorner shooting dice for nickels and
dimes, etc. (mere pittances) . . . gambling off the money
they should take home to feed their starving children or pay
their small rents, or very important needs, etc.

   Mama Lucy and I used to go out to Front of Town when
we were very young—among those produce places—where
they would throw away spoiled potatoes, onions into a big
barrel, and she and I among other kids used to raid those
barrels—cut off the spoiled parts and sell them to restau-
rants. There was a baker shop which sold two loafs of stale
bread for a nickle. They would do that to help the poor
children. They could always get filled up at least on bread.
Mama Lucy and me had to do it lots of times. Many kids
suffered from hunger. Their father could have done some
honest work for a change. *No*, they would not do that. It
would be too much like right. (*Archive*)

Those words and others far more bitter are balanced by
the dozens of pages in which he expresses gratitude to a
little-known family that he came to consider his salvation,
about whom he wrote, "If it wasn't for the nice Jewish people, we would have starved many times. I will love the Jewish
people all of my life." In an article he wrote for *True* in 1947,
Armstrong told of his first job, selling coal from a wagon
"for a young white boy whose folks had several wagons that
paraded all over the city. . . . They were the Karnoffsky [sic]

family." Their son Morris "liked the dickens outa me," he wrote, describing how they hustled coal to the prostitutes in Storyville. The "Karnoffskys" don't appear in his book on New Orleans. Yet in his last years, Armstrong wrote at length of a Karnofsky family, tracing their progress in the black section of New Orleans, the prejudice they faced, and the great wealth they ultimately achieved by buying property all over the South. He remained in contact with them for much of his life and it may be that after the *True* article, they asked him not to write of their déclassé start in and around the red-light district. Armstrong's 1969 memoir refutes at least two widely accepted details of his biography— that his first job was selling newspapers and that he obtained his first cornet in the Colored Waif's Home. He started working at the age of seven:

> The Karnofskys lived on the corner of Girod and Franklin Streets, one block away from the Girod Street Cemetery in the colored section. . . . Things were getting pretty rough for Mayann, me, and Mama Lucy, especially without a father. But we managed beautifully with the Karnofskys in my corner, and Mayann had her little hustle in the white folks yard. Mama Lou didn't work. The Karnofsky family came to America from somewhere in Russia long before I was born. They came to New Orleans as poor as Job's turkey. They settled in a neighborhood which was nothing but a gang of rundown houses with the privies out in the backyard. . . . They had a pretty good size yard, so they started a little business in no time at all. That's where I came in. With little money that they had, they bought two small

horses, two small wagons, harness for the horses. I alter-
nated with the two sons. One went out in the street, buying
old rags, bones, iron, bottles, any kind of old junk. Go back
to the house with the big yard, untie the wagon, pile up the
old rags in one place, the bottles, bones, and the rest of the
junk, all in separate places.

Soon there would be big piles of everything. There was
enough room for piles of stone coal which the older son,
Morris, sold in the streets also. Especially in the red-light
district, mostly in the evenings way into the night. He sold
it five cents a waterbucket to lots of the sporting women
standing in the doorways. Alex would go out early in the
mornings on his junk wagon—stay out all day, me right
alongside of him. Then I would help Morris at night. The
first job that I ever had, so I was very glad of it. . . . I began
to feel like I had a future and "It's a Wonderful World" after
all. (*Archive*)

At night, Mrs. Karnofsky would insist that Louis have dinner with them ("I still eat their food, matzos, my wife Lucille
keeps them in her breadbox"). Later, Mrs. Karnofsky taught
him to sing "Russian Lullabye"—"so soft and sweet, then
bid each other good night. They were always warm and kind
to me . . . something a kid could use at seven and just starting out in the world. . . . When I reached the age of eleven I
began to realize that it was the Jewish family who instilled in
me singing from the heart." By that time Mayann had
moved her family to Perdido Street, next door to where Uncle Ike, now a widower, and his two youngest sons had also
moved. They lived in one room; Louis and Mama Lucy

(who was assigned to sweep up) slept on a pallet on the floor, while Mayann and "stepfather" Tom Lee, who the kids liked, had the bed. "We had a great understanding, especially about sex time between Mayann and Tom," he wrote, describing the grunts he and Mama Lucy pretended not to hear in the darkness. Mayann had them say prayers every night and blessings before every meal. He always insisted that he never got out of the habit of bedtime prayer.

Louis developed a vocal quartet with his friends and they would harmonize for hours at a time on the street. According to the *True* article, they would scrape tins and blow harmonicas to draw a crowd. One boy performed an early form of breakdancing—standing on his head on a bean can, spinning around while the rest cried encouragement. Louis's first instrument was a tin horn that he had started playing on the Karnofsky rag wagon: "One day I took the wooden top right off the horn, and surprisingly I held my two fingers close together where the wooden mouthpiece used to be, and I could play a tune of some kind. Oh, the kids really enjoyed that." He was eleven and convinced he had "music in my soul."

> After blowing the tin horn so long I wondered how I would do blowing a real horn. A cornet was what I had in mind. Sure enough I saw a little cornet in a pawn shop window— five dollars. My luck was just right. With the Karnofskys loaning me on my salary, I saved fifty cents a week and bought the horn. All dirty—but was soon pretty to me. After blowing into it a while I realized that I could play "Home Sweet Home"—then here come the blues. From

then I was a mess and tootin' away. I kept that horn for a long time, I played it all through the days of the honky tonks. People thought that my first horn was given to me at the Colored Waif's Home for Boys (the orphanage). But it wasn't. (*Archive*)

This account confirms the widely disputed testimonies of Bunk Johnson, who (see William Russell's chapter in *Jazzmen*) insisted that Louis started playing in 1911, and of Sidney Bechet, who (in *Treat It Gentle*) also said he saw Louis with a cornet before he entered the Waif's Home.

In 1912, Louis had his sea change. He dropped out of school and quit working for the Karnofsky family. ("I became a little large for the job. Anyway they came into larger businesses.") He had long since become infatuated with the great musicians who played outside the tonks to draw a crowd, especially Joe Oliver, whom he idolized. Although his quartet was getting so good that established musicians, including Bechet, stopped by to hear him sing, he was undoubtedly frustrated in his desire to master the cornet. He begged for pointers and was usually sloughed off. He started getting into trouble. Things came to a head in the early hours of January 1, 1913, when he was out celebrating New Year's with friends. On a dare, he borrowed his stepfather's .38 revolver and fired six blanks into the air. He was collared for disturbing the peace and, after spending a night in jail, was remanded to the Colored Waif's Home for Boys. Under the direction of the sainted Captain Joseph Jones, a former cavalry officer and a legend among southern educators, the home was organized along strict military lines. Jones drilled the boys with wooden rifles, and discipline was absolute and often severe. Still, he instilled in them a sense of personal value, while other instructors offered vocational training in carpentry, gardening, and music.

Although records of the Waif's Home, which became part of the Milne Municipal Boys Home and as such survived until 1956, were apparently destroyed, Capt. Jones recalled at the end of his life that Armstrong was in custody at least twice. According to Joseph L. Peyton, the clerk of court for Orleans Parish Juvenile Court since 1940—and the successor in that job to his father, who had it from 1908—Louis was in and out of the Waif's Home during his early teenage years. Peyton says that Louis's chief crime was stealing newspapers from the white boys, who sold them on streetcars. That was a "white-only" job, he says, and whenever Louis was seen leaving a streetcar with papers under his arm, he was arrested and returned to the Waif's Home. Before long, Capt. Jones took him under his wing and got through to him. So did Peter Davis, who taught music and formed an orchestra.

Davis was wary of Louis at first, but after a six-month probation period permitted him to play tambourine, then alto horn, bugle, and finally cornet. Louis was proud of playing "Taps," and worked constantly at developing his embouchure. He cut grooves in the mouthpiece so it would hold to his mouth, and practiced every chance. Realizing he had an exceptional talent on his hands, Davis would occasionally take Louis home with him on his day off and allow him to play duets and sing hymns with his niece, Ida, a pianist. Louis responded to the discipline of the Waif's

Home—in later years he spoke of it warmly and made several low-key charitable visits; indeed, he was somewhat reluctant to leave when, in June 1914, he was released in care of his father. Not surprisingly, he didn't take to looking after Willie's "other" family and soon returned to Mayann and Mama Lucy.

Four

LOUIS SEEMS TO HAVE HAD NO TIME for repose as a child, and he never asked for any as an adult. At seventeen, he played parades with astonishing energy, earning the respect of older musicians as well as his contemporaries, who showered him with affectionate nicknames. "Even in my young days I accumulated several," he recalled in 1969. "Given by your little pals and people who like you . . . they all liked me and my cornet playing. Boy every time I looked around, somebody in some band had laid a new name on me. The Dippermouth is still around whenever I go to New Orleans and run into some of the old timers. Brings back real pleasant memories of the good old days. Here's some nicknames that very few fans I doubt ever heard of, such as Boat Note, Hammock Face, Rhythm Jaws." (*Archive*) He learned every theater and tonk in town as he felt his way through the underground that was black New Orleans.

To earn money, he took a grueling job driving a coal wagon and kept at it until the armistice in November 1918.

The day he heard of the peace, he "immediately dropped that shovel, slowly put on my jacket—looked at Lady [his mule], and said, 'So long, my dear, I don't think I'll ever see you again. . . .' I haven't seen them since." (*My*) Weeks later he married Daisy Parker, a prostitute who tried to hustle him at the Brick House, a cabaret in Gretna catering to longshoremen and, in Armstrong's words, "one of the toughest joints I ever played in." Writing in 1954, he recalled, "we were both young and giddy. Daisy was a brown-skinned girl and I was in love with her. She was a little skinny but she was cute. She was older than me and more experienced in the rough ways of the New Orleans tenderloin district." She was also insanely jealous and quick to bring out the razor she always carried. They soon separated, though the marriage lasted four years.

Before the year was out, Louis was living with Mayann while working at Tom Anderson's, "playing all sorts arrangements from the easiest to the hardest and from the sweetest to the hottest. T'was called jazz back there in those days. I was also doubling with the Tuxedo Brass Band." Things picked up now. He had a reputation for playing blues and an ingratiating manner, and he was never too tired to work. In 1916, Captain Joseph Streckfus experimented by putting black musicians on one of his steamers, the *S. S. Sydney*. At first jazz was kept to the upper deck, while a sweet band played on the lower, but it became so popular that he fired the fox-trotters. Fate Marable, a pianist who had played on riverboats since 1907 and was renowned for the way he manipulated the calliope that announced the ship's arrival in port, was put in charge of the band. One night he heard

Louis sitting in with Kid Ory's band at Co-operative Hall and decided he had to have him on the boat.

> Finally quit the band at Tom Anderson's to go on the boat—
> excursion boat called the *Steamer Sydney*. I joined Fate
> Marable's band. That's when—during our intermissions—he
> would help me out with my reading music. And me being a
> very apt young man I learned a whole lots of reading music
> real quick. Fate Marable was a good bandleader—and very
> strict on us when it came to playing the music right. He is
> absolutely responsible for a lot of youngsters' successes.
> (*Goffin*)

When people talk about jazz traveling up the river they are paying tribute to Marable, whether they know it or not. When the boat docked at various stopovers on the Mississippi, the robust piping of the calliope brought thousands of people to the river's edge to hear a music rarely played outside of New Orleans. The musicians who worked with Marable would play significant roles in jazz for decades to come, among them Baby Dodds, Johnny Dodds, Johnny St. Cyr, Pops Foster, Wellman Braud, Honore Dutrey, Red Allen, and David Jones, who also coached Louis with his reading. Among the young white musicians who heard Marable's men were Bix Beiderbecke and Jess Stacy. Jack Teagarden first heard Armstrong on the dock in New Orleans: "Suddenly, across the muddy waters of the Mississippi, came faint but bell-clear sounds of a high-pitched cornet . . . that cornet was filling the night with the hottest, the sweetest and purest jazz I'd ever heard."

Louis played excursions with Marable through the summer of 1921, but he also played the New Orleans cabarets in those years. The best band in the opinion of many was the one Joe Oliver and Kid Ory led together. In early 1918 Oliver, like many musicians before him, moved to Chicago; several months later, Ory asked Louis to take his place. That offer crystallized his position as the most esteemed of the young players. He boasted a resplendent tone and an irresistible ebullience even then. He was considered prodigious and he knew it. Most of the players, he wrote in 1969, "were fading out—some of them were still pretty good, but nothing like when they were in their heydays. Maybe it was because most of them worked too hard doing other hard jobs such as longshoreman on the docks all day, unloading ships, and lots of other hard labor which kept them too tired to even look at their instruments let alone play it, which makes them rusty."

In 1921, the young Fletcher Henderson, who was touring the South as Ethel Waters's pianist, heard Louis and tried to lure him to New York, where he intended to organize an orchestra. Louis begged off, saying he didn't want to leave his band. But a year later, when his mentor and idol King Oliver wired him to come to Chicago, Louis left with alacrity. On the afternoon of August 8, four days after his twenty-first birthday, he played a funeral with the Tuxedo Jazz Band, packed a small bag, including a trout sandwich his mother had fixed, and caught the evening train.

Five

THE LINCOLN GARDENS CAFE on Chicago's South Side was a large balconied ballroom with a revolving cut-glass ball that refracted the light. It became famous in 1922, when King Oliver brought in his Creole Jazz Band. He is said to have earned his sobriquet by cutting Freddie Keppard one night in Storyville, but it didn't stick until he made his reputation up north. At thirty-seven, he was a stern taskmaster but a rather genteel man, loyal to his home boys (as Louis was), and ready—with twenty years of playing behind him— for the big time. The band he presented on opening night, June 17, was made up of men from New Orleans: trombonist Honore Dutrey, clarinetist Johnny Dodds, bassist and banjoist Bill Johnson, drummer Baby Dodds, plus pianist Bertha Gonsoulin from California. By the time he sent for Louis, he had replaced the pianist with another woman, Memphis-born Lil Hardin. Louis said later (see Appendix) that the band sounded so fine the night he arrived, he didn't think he was good enough to play with it. But when he opened formally the next night, he knew he was home:

> The first number went down so well we had to take [an] encore, that was the moment Joe Oliver and I developed a little system whereby we didn't have to write down the duet breaks. I was so wrapped up in him and lived his music that I could take second to his lead in a split second. (*My*)

Oliver and his wife found him a place to live and taught him the ways of Chicago. Within weeks, Louis got hold of a typewriter and began writing his old friends. The earliest surviving letter (in the Jazz Archive at Tulane University) was written September 1, 1922, to the veteran brassman Isadore Barbarin, whose son, drummer Paul Barbarin, was a contemporary, friend, and bandmate of Louis's.

Mr. Barbarin.
    Dear Friend.
    Yours of this afternoon has been received. And I take great pleasure in letting you know that I was glad to hear from you. I'm well as usual and also doing fine as usual. Hoping you and family are well. Pops I just had started to wondering what was the matter with you. You takin' so long to answer: Well I know just how it is when a fellow is play-ing with a red hot brass band and they have all the work he don't have time to be bothered with writing no letters.
    Well I understand that Pops. I heard all about you all having all those funerals down there. I'm sorry that I ain't down there to make some of them with you all. The boys

give me H . . . all the time because [I'm] forever talking about the Brass Band and how I used to like to make those parades. They say I don't see how a man can be crazy about those hard parades. I told them that they don't go hard with you when you are playing with a good band. Joe Oliver is here in my room now and he sends you his best regards. Also all the boys. I heard the Celestin lost his sister. Well that's too bad. I feel sorry for the poor fellow. I will tell Paul what you said when I see him again. The next time you meet Nenest ask him what is the matter with him he don't answer my letter. Ask him [if] he needs any writing paper-stamps to let me know at once and I'll send him some at once . . Ha . . Ha . . Well old pal I tell you the news some other time. I have to go to work now. Good knight.

All from Louis Armstrong. 459 East 31 St. Chicago, Ill.

I choose to believe that the closer is a pun rather than a spelling error, of which the letter has several. In any case, the use of "Pops" indicates Armstrong's talent for coining slang. Baby Dodds later said that he'd never heard such phrases as "you cats" and "look out there Pops" in New Orleans until Armstrong started using them on the bandstand. Among the words that Louis is believed to have coined or popularized in his early years are several that became part of the English language: *chops*, *jive*, *scat*, *gutbucket*, *mellow*, and *solid* (as terms of approbation), and *Pops*, *Face*, and *Daddy* (as forms of address). He's even been credited with the hoariest of all bandleader puns, "not too fast, not too slow, just half-fast," perhaps because he had the brass to use it on network radio and television.

The Armstrong discography begins with the recordings of King Oliver's Creole Jazz Band—thirty-seven performances (many other takes were made but destroyed) waxed between April and December 1923. The most enduring tale of those sessions tells how Armstrong had to play twenty feet behind the rest of the band, because his huge sound overwhelmed the ensemble and recording equipment. True or not, Armstrong made an impression—despite his role as second cornet to Oliver's lead and the absence of solo space. The polyphonic New Orleans style, which Oliver honed to perfection, was not designed to parade the skills of virtuoso soloists. Two years later, Armstrong would ignite the revolution that established jazz as a soloist's art. With Oliver, however, he had to prove himself a team player. Despite restraints, the young man, whom Oliver introduced as his adopted son, made an astonishing debut on records. One need not have a trained ear to be taken aback by his virtually "straight" readings of the trio themes on "Froggy Moore" and especially "Chimes Blues." His declamatory tone and rhythmic dash are unmistakable. His best work with Oliver came at subsequent sessions—his breaks on "Tears," which prefigure his mature style; his full chorus and coda on the sublime "Riverside Blues"; the thrusting counterpoint between the two cornets on "Mabel's Dream"; and the celebrated double-cornet breaks on "Snake Rag," "Buddy's Habits," "Where Did You Stay Last Night?" and two incomparable examples of collective propulsion, "Chattanooga Stomp" and "I Ain't Gonna Tell Nobody."

Louis was also getting a feel for show business, mustering the self-confidence that would eventually allow him to con-

quer the stage in Chicago and New York. One source of inspiration was his favorite entertainer, Bill Robinson, the subject of an enlightening homage:

He was the sharpest Negro man that I personally [have]
ever seen in my life onstage, since the first time that I ever
laid eyes on him at the Erlanger Theater in Chicago in
1922. I had just come up from New Orleans. . . . I had Bill
Johnson, who had been on the RKO Circuit, take me to the
matinee show one day so I could see this man whom I had
heard and read about in my early days in N.O. Bojangles
came up to every expectation and opinion that I had of him
before I saw him in person. I am sitting in my seat in the
theater, very anxious to see this man, and sure enough the
great one appeared. As he came out of the wing onstage, the
first thing that hit him was the flashlight. Sharp—Lord
knows that man was so sharp he was bleeding (our expression when we mention someone that's well dressed)—
Anyway he had on a sharp light tan gabardine summer suit,
brown derby, and the usual thick-soul shoes in which he
tapped.

It was a long time before Bojangles could open his
mouth. That's how popular he was and well-liked by all who
understood his greatness as a dancer and a showman. He
waited after the thunderous applause had finished, and
looked up into the booth and said to the man who controlled the lights—Bill said to him, "Give me a light, *My*
color." And all the lights all over the house went out. And
me sitting there when this happened, with the whole audience just roaring with laughter. When I realized it, I was

laughing so loud, until Bill Johnson was on the verge of taking me out of there. I hadn't heard anything like that before or witnessed it either. Then Bojangles went into his act. His every move was a beautiful picture. I am sitting in my seat in ecstasy and delight, even in a trance. He imitated a trombone with his walking cane to his mouth, blowing out of the side of his mouth making the buzzing sound of a trombone, which I enjoyed. He told a lot of funny jokes, which everybody enjoyed immensely. Then he went into his dance and finished by skating off of the stage with a silent sound and tempo. *Wow* what an artist. I was sold on him ever since. (*Archive*)

In February 1924, Armstrong married Lil Hardin, who voiced impatience with Louis's second-banana loyalty to King Oliver. For his part, he was infatuated with the idea of winning the hand of so sophisticated a woman—educated, older, and desired by everyone in the band:

From the first night on the bandstand I noticed that all of the boys in Joe's band had been very busy trying to make a play for Lil, who was the Belle of the Windy City of Chicago at that time. Well, as for me, I was wrapped up in music and did not pay any attention at first to the fact that Lil was stuck on me. But who was I to think that a big high-powered chick like Lillian Hardin who came to Chicago from Memphis, Tenn.—the year of 1917—right out of Fisk University—Valedictorian of her classes—Who me?—I thought to myself. I just couldn't conceive the idea—that's all. (*Goffin*)

The other band members grumbled with jealousy—one of them called Armstrong "a country sonbitch" for courting her—but Louis and Lil confided in each other about their bad first marriages, and when Mayann visited Chicago and gave her approval, they filed their respective divorces and married. With Lil on his arm, Louis began acting the sport, taking her to the Dreamland Cafe and tipping May Alix and Ollie Powers to sing for them. One musician they went to hear was an old rival of King Oliver's, Freddie Keppard, and Armstrong was not impressed. Armstrong's subsequent criticism of Keppard is ironic in light of attacks with which he would later be plagued:

> Freddie Keppard slipped out of the scene into oblivion. A
> heavy drinker. His ego when he was a young man and
> [the] clowning that he did must have been rather amusing
> for laughs, to get the recognition he achieved. But he
> sure did not play the cornet seriously at any time. Just
> clowned all the way. Good for those idiot fans, who did not
> care whether he played correct. . . . The first time I heard
> Freddie Keppard at an after hours joint was on the South-
> side of Chicago, he did not move me at all. He played a lot
> of almost high drunken notes. (*Archive*)

In 1969 he also had harsh words for the woman pianist who had tried to convince him that Keppard had a better tone than Oliver. He was upset because "she did not know jazz [but] had the nerve to accept the title as a piano player, and at the same time sitting in bands with the most fa- mous jazz men in the world! How she got that job—that I

can't figure out until this day. . . . Read music, yes—as an
improviser—hmm—terrible. . . . This chick admits all she
was interested in was the paydays, more money than she's
ever made. Am sure she hasn't made near that much salary
since the band broke up. Because music is much more modern nowadays and she was corny then. Guess who?" It's hard
not to guess he was referring to Lil Hardin, though they
maintained a cordial relationship until his death. Musically,
his assessment of Lil isn't too surprising; but his candor indicates his lasting loyalty to Oliver and his ambivalence about
leaving him at Lil's insistence. She convinced him to accept
an offer from Fletcher Henderson, and he headed for New
York.

The spell Armstrong cast on the best musicians in New
York can hardly be overestimated. Only one other soloist in
jazz history, Charlie Parker, in the 1940s, would ever cast so
wide a net over every breed of musician. Like Parker,
Armstrong was perceived as a rube, an ignorant country boy
with a funny manner. A widely told story found him ignor-
ing a *pp* marking during rehearsal. Henderson stops the
band and asks him if he knows what *pp* (*pianissimo*—very
softly) means. "Yes sir," Louis announces. "Pound plenty!"
Musicians didn't laugh long—they were too busy overhaul-
ing their styles to match the rube's heady rhythms, blues
sensibility, and incomparable sense of proportion.

Every great improviser is a great editor. It's easy to run
scales up and down the horn; but picking out the notes that
mean something is hard. Interpreting a phrase in a way that
makes it personal is the mark of a master. Louis's ability to
project feeling and his innate sense of musical logic were

modern in ways that made everyone else sound fussy and antiquated. He taught New York to swing. Danny Barker, the New Orleans–born guitarist who later toured with Armstrong's big band, has suggested that Armstrong's greatest achievement was to jettison the jaunty second-line two-beat rhythm of New Orleans in favor of the evenly distributed four-four beat that is the basis of swing. Indeed, the swing era has been characterized as orchestrated Armstrong.

When Louis joined Henderson, the orchestra specialized in commercial pieces—fox-trots and waltzes for the dancers at the Roseland Ballroom, as well as self-consciously crafted jazz numbers. Henderson's ingenious arranger, Don Redman, and such instrumentalists as saxophonist Coleman Hawkins and clarinetist Buster Bailey (whom Louis had known in Chicago and recommended to Henderson) were well-schooled virtuosi who listened closely to the records coming out of Chicago. But the orchestra's early spin-offs, though deferential, lacked the tang of authenticity. Armstrong's spellbinding improvisations served as antidotes to the baroque doodling, plodding time, and overwritten arrangements of the day. They are the sparkplugs that start the ensemble throbbing on "Go Long Mule," "Copenhagen," and—not withstanding his difficulties with a plunger mute (a technique made famous by Oliver but rejected by Armstrong)—"Shanghai Shuffle." Louis's stirring chorus on "One of These Days" and his theme statement on "Everybody Loves My Baby" are savory moments in otherwise leaden performances. The pioneering Don Redman admitted, "I changed my style of arranging after I heard Louis Armstrong." Who could resist his passion and robust attack?

Yet not even Henderson was prepared to let the complete Armstrong come through. Although the brief scat break at the close of "Everybody Loves My Baby" marks Louis's recorded debut as a singer, he was not allowed to sing on-stage, let alone on other Henderson records.

Not the least refreshing aspect of the sojourn with Fletcher was the chance to travel. After six months at the Roseland, the band toured New England. "We were the first colored big band to hit the road," Armstrong wrote Goffin. "We went all through the New England states. We spent our first summer up in Lawrence, Mass." On days off, he and Buster Bailey would go swimming—"one of my famous hobbies," he noted, "outside of typing." Still, he never for-got Henderson's refusal to let him sing. In a privately recorded discussion in 1960 (which shows, as his public writings often do not, how confident he was of his talent and potential commercial value), he told Fred Rabell, "Fletcher didn't dig me like Joe Oliver. He had a million-dollar talent in his band and he never thought enough to let me sing or nothing. He'd go hire a singer that lived up in Harlem that night for a recording next day who didn't even know the song. And I'd say, 'Let me sing.' But no, all he had was the trumpet in mind, and that's why he missed the boat." That's one reason he left Henderson after fourteen months, having made nearly forty records with him. He was also feeling pressure from Lil to come home to Chicago. She was get-ting jealous, and with good reason. Louis was in great de-mand in and out of the studios. His recording activities in New York were by no means confined to the Henderson band.

An exceptional series of records by the Clarence Williams Blue Five combined the breezy entertainment of vaudeville (vocals by Eva Taylor and Virginia Liston) with the sweeping exuberance of a lean New Orleans–style cabaret band. They paired Louis with the only man who, for a very short while, seemed his equal as an improviser in those transitional years, soprano saxophonist and clarinetist Sidney Bechet. The highlights include Armstrong's impeccable lead and slashing breaks on "Cake Walking Babies from Home" and his note-bending and call-and-response with the reeds on "Papa De-Da-Da." Above all there is his explosive chorus on the Blue Five version of "Everybody Loves My Baby," in which he uses a plunger mute in homage to Oliver, ripping and snorting against the beat, accenting against expectations (for example, the fourth beat of the tenth measure), raising the roof during the stoptime release, and growling his way into the last eight bars. The record was a huge success and the talk of Harlem. Some of the lyrics from those sessions also attracted attention: "Pickin' on Your Baby," a mild protest piece about a pickaninny rose, offers sly contrast with the Fanny Brice hit "Second Hand Rose" (1921), and "I'm a Little Blackbird" archly advocates miscegenation.

The stopper was still on, though: The full radiance of Louis's music and personality was simmering, waiting for release. But his reputation spread among musicians and producers, and he never had to ask for work. His three numbers with Ma Rainey and Her Georgian Jazz Band (actually a pickup ensemble from the Henderson Orchestra) demonstrate the sensitivity, economy, and forthrightness that made his obbligati so highly valued. His most successful collaboration was with the Empress of the Blues, Bessie Smith. He said of their nine sides together, "She'd always have the words and tune in her head, and we'd just run it down once. Then she'd sing a few lines, and I'd play something to fill it in, and some nice beautiful notes behind her. Everything I did with her, I *like*." Other sessions with singers in New York and Chicago were less consistently good but constitute a relatively little known cache of important early Louis. The variety of material is impressive—fast blues, slow blues, vaudeville novelties, basic pop. The singers were usually billed as blues divas, but many weren't, and only a few sustain interest in their own right—notably Bertha Hill, Sippie Wallace, Hociel Thomas, and Clara Smith. Yet Louis, brimming with energy, rarely let the singer or the material get him down.

One amusing session starred Lillie Delk Christian, a justly obscure cabaret singer whose vibrato quivered as fast and furious as Alvin and the Chipmunks'. The best of the eight sides she cut in 1928 with Armstrong's Hot 4 is "Too Busy": She trudges through the sappy tune without the remotest suggestion of swing, but after an instrumental interlude, Armstrong sneaks up on her with some impromptu scat that swings so hard you can almost hear Lillie's stomach rising. Bertha "Chippie" Hill, on the other hand, was a genuine blues singer, and Armstrong obviously enjoyed working with her. The material is excellent and his cogent fills on "Lonesome Weary Blues" and "Low Land Blues" rival his work with Bessie Smith. The Sippie Wallace sessions benefit from the presence of her teenage brother, pianist Hersal Thomas, whose backup on "Special Delivery Blues" anticipates Thelonious Monk's "Blue Monk." Margaret Johnson's "Changeable Daddy," Eva Taylor's "You Can't Shush Katie," and Hociel Thomas's "Sunshine Baby" are among the other worthy sides from Armstrong's apprenticeship as a sideman.

Six

Lil had a place for him in her band at the Dreamland Cafe (at seventy-five dollars a week) when Louis returned to Chicago. Fletcher had thrown him a lavish going-away party, assuring him a spot in the band if ever he wished to return (despite Louis's getting drunk at the party and throwing up on Henderson's tux). For a while Armstrong figured he would return, since Lil's band seemed such a comedown after "Fletcher and his fine band," but he soon realized he was building a reputation in Chicago worth nurturing.

> I had become so popular at the Dreamland [that] Erskine
> Tate from the Vendome Theater came to hire me to join his
> Symphony Orchestra. I like to have fainted. Erskine Tate
> had a 20 piece orch playing at a moving picture house called
> the Vendome Theater located at 31st and State Streets in
> Chicago. In those days they had silent films instead of the
> talkies. His Orchestra would furnish the music for all the

scenes in the films. And when the picture would break the
Orchestra'd play overtures etc., and then they'd finish with a
red hot number—then blackout—then the picture would
start over again. . . . So when Erskine Tate came for me [I'd
been trying] to get the experience of playing classic and
symphony music, etc. Well, here's your chance, I said, ask
Lil. She said, "Boy, if you don't get out of this house and go
on down there to Erskine Tate's rehearsal, I'll skin you
alive." I said, slowly, "Well, all right, I'll go." I went down
there and the opening night was sensational. I remember
the first "swing tune" we played, called "Spanish Shawl." I
wasn't in Tate's Orch 2-weeks before I was making records
with them for the Vocalion Recording Company. I became
quite a figure at the Vendome. Especially with the gals.
(*Goffin*)

One of the gals was a nineteen-year-old named Alpha
Smith, for whom he eventually divorced Lil. He had become
a figure with the guys, too, especially young black musicians.
When the lights went down for the musical interludes, the
audience could see his trumpet poking above the pit; his solos got tremendous ovations. Tate would arrange for Armstrong to have a different specialty number every week. Doc
Cheatham, who switched from saxophone to cornet after
seeing Armstrong at the Vendome, recalls that as soon as the
"spotlight hit Louis for his feature, man, the people were
screaming so much you couldn't hear what he was playing
half the time." On several occasions, Armstrong asked
Cheatham to sub for him. The first time the spot hit
Cheatham, the audience went wild—until everyone realized

it wasn't Louis. "You could just measure the diminishing of the screams, right down to nothing," Cheatham recalled, "and I'm up there playing like a fool." While at the Vendome, Armstrong started playing trumpet as well as cornet, possibly at Tate's suggestion, though he continued to use both instruments through 1927. It's impossible to distinguish between the two on old records, but the trumpet is said to have a more brilliant tone, due in part to the design of the tubing, which gives it a longer, sleeker look.

On November 12, 1925, Armstrong made his first recordings as a leader. The session was the beginning of a monumental series that would last through 1928 and produce sixty-five performances for OKeh Records. Had he stopped performing at the end of 1928, Armstrong would never have become an international celebrity, an ambassador of jazz and goodwill, a media star, a folk hero, and more. But he would still be regarded as the single most creative and innovative force in jazz history. Notwithstanding a handful of trite numbers and the intrusion of some vaudeville hokum, the OKeh recordings are no more dated—which is to say, diminished in the power to enlighten and astonish—than Bach cantatas. With Armstrong, jazz was in the hands of a virtuoso instrumentalist whose vision transcended the limitations of what was construed as pop music. Armstrong's genius surmounted everything, from poor material and uninspired associates to the constraints of recording technology and the winds of fashion. Here was unexampled expressive power in a new, authentically American mode. Even the nature of his virtuosity was sui generis: This was not a man who could interpret the Haydn trumpet concerto, but an artist who produced a tone of insuperable brilliance and improvised musical statements that are as logical and emotionally satisfying as any written score.

To say that Armstrong and his music were not appreciated as such by the academy or the white public is to belabor the obvious. In the 1920s, jazz was excoriated from the pulpit, blamed by women's groups for the increase in rape, belittled by intellectuals and musicologists, scorned as whorehouse music, and worse. This was a music innovated by blacks without the benefit of a conservatory imprimatur. As such, it affronted the generation of New England humanists who were self-consciously attempting to do for American music what Whitman had done for American poetry—give it a New World voice. When the man who embodied that voice made himself known (in sweet guttural tones), they saw to their dismay a smiling Negro with a trumpet and repaired to their ivory-covered dens, hoping he would go away. Devoted black urban audiences, augmented by a handful of whites, kept the music alive in a difficult period. Armstrong had no nationwide following as of 1926, but records on which he appeared were selling in large numbers. Among the bestselling "race" records of 1925 and 1926—all featuring Armstrong—were Bessie Smith's "St. Louis Blues," Clarence Williams's "Everybody Loves My Baby" and "Cake Walking Babies," Fletcher Henderson's "Sugar Foot Stomp," and his own recordings of "Heebie Jeebies," "Muskrat Ramble," and "Cornet Chop Suey."

Like King Oliver's Creole Jazz Band, Armstrong's Hot 5 consisted of Orleanians—Johnny Dodds, Kid Ory, Johnny St. Cyr—plus Lil. Unlike Oliver's band, the Hot 5 and its successors (the Hot 7 and the Savoy Ballroom Five) existed only to make records. Armstrong continued to appear with stage orchestras. The primary difference between the Oliver and Armstrong records (the Clarence Williams sessions can be seen as transitional here) is the changeover from a group effort, where polyphony dominates, to a music for soloists. Modest embellishment gives way to daring improvisation, two- and four-bar breaks are expanded into solos of a full chorus or more, and the multiple refrains of ragtime composition are winnowed down to the cyclical choruses of popular songs and the blues. Armstrong was lucky to be recording for OKeh, which employed the best sound techs in the business. But he was nervous that first day, and the Hot 5 got off to an orderly but conservative start, recording three numbers: In "My Heart," Armstrong's solo pivots on a lick that prefigures by five years the pop song "Them There Eyes"; "Yes I'm in the Barrel" opens with an evocative riff before moving into tempo; and "Gut Bucket Blues" boasts a compelling Armstrong solo plus his genial verbal introductions of the musicians. It was a warm-up session.

At a far more productive second date the following February, the Hot 5 came into its own with a double-sided hit in "Heebie Jeebies" and "Muskrat Ramble." The first is famous for the impetuous vocal that put scat singing on the map and fostered countless imitations. Armstrong always insisted that the sheet music slipped from the stand and he started scatting to save the take. His unforgettable vocal is the high point of an otherwise uninspired performance, and it is hard to believe he did not know exactly what he was doing. That chorus did more than introduce a language of nonsense syllables that jazz singers could use when a song's lyric proved too constricting; it embodied a joyous, vernacular, and convincing attitude that complemented the spontaneous nature of the new music. Young singers didn't merely ape the idea—they wanted Armstrong's gravelly voice as well. It would be another four years before singers realized how versatile his voice was, but from the moment Louis's "novelty" vocal hit the streets, other musicians were, in Earl Hines's recollection, sticking their heads out of windows trying to catch colds to sound like Louis. The flip side, "Muskrat Ramble," became an immediate jazz standard (so enduringly popular that a rock 'n' roll version ensued in the early sixties). Another piece, "Oriental Strut," incorporated 1920s exotica, an "Oh, By Jingo!"–inspired vamp, and stoptime—a common gambit in which the soloist improvises freely while one or more members of the band seem to stop the flow of time with a unison stomping on certain beats. The accents might fall on the first beat of alternate measures, for example, or on the first three beats of every measure.

The breakthrough performance of the session was the beaming "Cornet Chop Suey." Here the soloist is paramount, and the other horns less a partnership in the front line than a backup, trying to keep up. Excepting a piano solo, Armstrong is the whole show, from the martial introduction through an exciting sixteen-bar passage of stoptime breaks to a chorus of elegantly phrased eighth-note figures with melodic ideas that were widely imitated for years. Louis later said he wrote "Cornet Chop Suey" sitting on a staircase during a break on a jaunt around Chicago.

The masterpiece by the original Hot 5 personnel was made twenty months later, by which time Louis was a studio veteran. The tantalizing melody of "Struttin' with Some Barbecue" is built on a major seventh in a way that prefigures "Samba de Orpheus," the Brazilian hit of forty years later. Although the performance is carefully arranged with an introduction, varied backups for the three soloists (Dodds and Ory split a chorus), and unison figures, the performance is a showcase for the entertainer as artist, flaunting his brilliance with mercurial rips, dazzling triplets, a glissando that seems to swallow its own tail. The twelve-bar intro precedes a traditional theme statement, but Armstrong's improvisation stops tradition in its tracks: Accompanied by banjo accents on the offbeats, he arcs over the ensemble, defying gravity and bar lines.

Like Paganini, Armstrong embodies the musician as sprite. Yet his presentation is underscored by a canny ingenuousness that is without precedent or equal. Like a prodigious child showing off for the grown-ups, Armstrong invites us to participate in the celebration of his gift. Whether the invitation is made explicit in spoken remarks that puncture any trace of solemnity about the artist's role or is conveyed through the sheer bravura of his instrumental technique, a democratization of artist and audience takes place. He looks us right in the eye, evoking the promise of a common clay, as if to say, "Now dig this," before blowing us away with a mastery that is awesome but never intimidating. The generosity of his impulse as an artist/entertainer made the Hot 5 and 7 possible and guaranteed his later triumphs as an ambassador of the musical world he created.

His disarming street-smart liberality came to the fore at the December 1927 session, when the Hot 5 recorded three sides with a guest musician, guitarist Lonnie Johnson, who would enjoy a second career in the postwar era as a blues singer. In the 1920s, he was much admired by jazz musicians for his jaunty counterpoint to Baby Cox's vocal on Ellington's "The Mooche," his triplets on the initial recordings of the Chocolate Dandies, his duets with Eddie Lang, a white guitarist who adopted a pseudonym (Blind Willie Dunn) for the occasion, and his appearance with the Hot 5. Johnson plays a pivotal role on Armstrong's "I'm Not Rough," shadowing the three-chorus trumpet solo with trills, providing the sole accompaniment for the vocal, and bearing down in the final passages with fourth-beat accents. His startling solo is made up entirely of evenly articulated triplets, foreshadowing the rhythms of rock 'n' roll. He seems to spur Armstrong to a new level of abandon—one that nearly upsets the band's balance on the engaging but less forceful "Savoy Blues."

The best of the Armstrong-Johnson records is the ingenious "Hotter Than That," based on a strain of "Tiger Rag." After the introduction, Louis romps through the theme, bursting into a two-bar break at bar fifteen, the melodic content of which appeared in many guises during the next decade (the Ink Spots sing it on "Java Jive"). What should have been Armstrong's second break (at bar thirty-one) functions instead as a relay point—Johnny Dodds begins his chorus by bagging that break. In the same fashion,

Armstrong picks up from Dodds to begin an improbably complex scat chorus, highlighted with devious cross-rhythms. His finest vocal to date, it was a stunning example of a musician superimposing one rhythm over another, and its implications ran deep. (Compare Miles Davis's similar gambit in the first four bars of his second chorus of "No Blues" on *At Carnegie Hall.*) Then he vocally exchanges two-bar phrases with Johnson's guitar, anticipating the duet for voice and clarinet in the 1928 "West End Blues." After a trombone solo, Armstrong's trumpet explodes with a break and improvisation capped with twelve high-Cs spaced over seven bars. "Hotter Than That" is three minutes of daunting surprises.

Armstrong's energy level seems all the more remarkable if you take into account that in 1926, he was working day and night. He played four shows at the Vendome, finishing at eleven, then went over to the Sunset Cafe, where he was featured in the big band led by Carroll Dickerson. Switching from Lil's band at the Dreamland to the Sunset was necessary, since he was now spending much of his time and money on Alpha. It was notable for other reasons. The Sunset was owned by Joe Glaser, a mob-connected promoter whose eventual partnership with Armstrong would make one an international star and the other an internationally powerful booking czar. In the 1920s, Glaser wasn't interested in personal management, and Louis was doing well on his own.

Wow was I making nice money so I had a good chance to buy Alpha some nice things with my extra money Lil didn't

> know about. . . . I used to love to take her out on Sunday
> and we would drive out to Blue Island. Bill Bottoms (Joe
> Louis's ex-dietician) was the owner of the roadhouse out
> there, and Alpha, me, Tubby Hall, who was the drummer in
> Carroll Dickerson's band at the time, and his girl—the four
> of us would drive out in my brand new Ford car with the
> yellow wire wheels. (*Goffin*)

Alpha turned out to be interested primarily in "furs and
diamonds"—"a no good bitch," in Armstrong's final estimation. The Sunset, however, turned out to be a godsend.
Early in 1927, Glaser fired Dickerson, who had a drinking
problem, and turned the band over to Louis. He was now
fronting his first band at a major club, surrounded by some
of the best players in Chicago, including pianist Earl Hines.
It was at the Sunset Cafe that Louis's irrepressible gifts as an
entertainer really blossomed; on some evenings, he would
don an old black, box-back deacon's coat and sermonize as
the Reverend Satchelmouth. Among the most devoted
members of his audience were musicians from the Paul
Whiteman Orchestra who came to hear his last set when
their own shows were over. None was more attentive than
Whiteman's singer, Bing Crosby, who began a long friendship with Louis that proved mutually inspiring. Nine years
later, Bing would use his clout in Hollywood to commence
Louis's film career, which established him as a national
celebrity.

For a while the OKeh recording setup remained the same,
though he made some changes for a few sessions in May,
replacing Ory with John Thomas, and adding Pete Briggs,

who played tuba in the Sunset band, and drummer Baby Dodds, his old friend from the riverboats. The Hot 7, as the new group was called, recorded eleven titles, demonstrating a substantially richer texture and a more provocative and assured Armstrong. The irresistible "Potato Head Blues," its valorous theme evoking the brass band roots of New Orleans jazz, is the band's seminal performance. A highly charged Johnny Dodds solo and a banjo break herald Armstrong, who struts through his stoptime chorus with a certitude that borders on arrogance. It's a rousing celebration of self, underscored by searing emotion. His syncopations are dazzling; his lead work in the final chorus is musical ecstasy. One of the record's admirers was Tallulah Bankhead, who insisted on playing it onstage for the three years she starred on Broadway in *Private Lives*. "It is one of the greatest things in life, in case anyone who is uninitiated to the true jazz wants to dig a great example of Louis," she wrote, "and while it may seem incongruous to put such a record in a Noel Coward drawing room comedy, I just had to have a snatch of Satch to alleviate the tedium of playing the same part for so long."

The boldness of Armstrong's and Dodds's solos dominate "Wild Man Blues," for which Armstrong shared composer credit with Jelly Roll Morton, though he attributed the melody to Morton. "S.O.L. Blues" and "Gully Low Blues" are two versions of the same piece (the former was suppressed until 1940, because of its lyric and shit-out-of-luck acronym), each noted for Armstrong's fierce descending arpeggios. "Weary Blues" begins with a fiery solo by Dodds and a punchy one by Thomas and peaks with a flamboyant

Armstrong takeoff that lands him in unexpectedly high terrain. Baby Dodds's cymbal-whacking ignites the finale of "Willie the Weeper"; "Twelfth Street Rag" succeeds in modernizing a piece that seemed naïvely raggy even in 1927; "Melancholy" has a lovely melody, reminiscent of "I Ain't Got Nobody," and a variation by the trumpeter that is lovelier still.

A significant indication of Louis's preeminence in 1927, at least among jazz and trumpet enthusiasts, was the publication of two books by the Melrose Bros. Music Company in Chicago: *Louis Armstrong's 50 Hot Choruses for Cornet* and *Louis Armstrong's 125 Jazz Breaks for Cornet.* The Foreword in both volumes accurately boasted, "Hundreds of jazz cornetists, who, by the way, are an important feature in all jazz orchestras, have adopted the Armstrong style of playing. . . . His ability is enthusiastically endorsed by all the great and near great." The books are of much value. As the Foreword explains, "The solos in this book depart in principle of production from any solos on the market. They are genuine inspirations obtained, not by the old method of the artist writing down his solos one note at a time, but from actual recordings. Special phonograph recording apparatus was employed to make them. They are red hot inspirations extracted from red hot jazz recordings." In other words, the solos were created exclusively for publication. Incredibly, the Edison cylinders on which Armstrong recorded them were destroyed, so all we have are the published transcriptions. (Bent Persson, a Swedish trumpeter and bandleader, has recorded four record albums that employ all the transcribed solos and breaks in the context of simulated Hot 5 and Hot 7 performances.) Still, they constitute a significant part of Armstrong's output in the 1920s, displaying his facility at improvising variations on dozens of tunes that he never otherwise recorded or, most likely, played—including Morton compositions, New Orleans pieces, and pop songs.

Seven

FOR A SHORT WHILE, ARMSTRONG found himself hustling for work again. He had quit the Vendome in April 1927, and in July the Sunset Cafe went dark. After a few unsuccessful gigs, he teamed up with Earl Hines and Zutty Singleton to hustle jobs.

> Earl, Zutty, and I stayed out of work so long until it was impossible for me to get my car out of the shop, even after it was fixed. Things [had] gotten so tough with us until fifteen cents looked like fifteen dollars. But we did not lose our spirit, and we all kept that ol' clean shirt on everyday, and ol' Earl Hines kept the big fresh cigar in his mouth everyday. Zutty and I both admired that. We were still riding in this "Pneumonia Special." That's the name we gave this hauling car. You'd be surprised to know how happy we were. (*Goffin*)

The three men even rented a dance hall on the West Side, called the Usonia, and drew pretty good crowds until a drunk came in one night and shot up the place. At the same time the Savoy Ballroom opened nearby and "was doing all the business in town." After the dance hall went bust, Louis was in hock as well as out of work. Fortunately for him, the Savoy fired the original house bands, led by Charles Elgar and Clarence Black—"two good bands," Armstrong recalled, that "would cut any band that came to the Savoy for one night"—and hired his old boss, Carroll Dickerson.

> Carroll had all the old timers rejoin him. Of course, Earl
> Hines couldn't make it, on account he had just given Jimmie
> Noone his word to play in his little four piece combination
> down at the Apex nightclub on 35th St. So Carroll hired
> Jean Anderson on piano. . . . But just the same with Jean,
> Zutty, Fred Robinson, Homer Hobson, Jimmy Strong,
> [Bert] Curry, Crawford Wethington, Peter Briggs, Mancy
> "Peck" Cara, Louis Armstrong, and Carroll Dickerson him-
> self, if I have to say it myself, we made up one of the
> damnedest bands there were. . . . (*Goffin*)

Louis was not yet twenty-seven in July 1928, but he considered himself one of the "old-timers" on the Chicago music scene and was especially pleased when Dickerson's men went into the Savoy and cut the "young boys" in "Clarence Black's band down to a low gravy." Adding insult to injury, they also whipped Black's men in a basketball game. "We'd just finished recording, etc. So it all turned out just fine—

then we became the favorite band of the house also."
(*Goffin*)

Louis was justly buoyed by those recordings. After six
months away from the studio, he had returned with Hines
and several members of the Dickerson band. At five sessions
recorded between June 26 (the spunky date with Lillie Delk
Christian) and July 5 (the entire Dickerson band), he sur-
passed everything he'd already done. The group was still
called the Hot 5, though it was a sextet, and if Jimmy
Strong, Fred Robinson, and Mancy Cara weren't as accom-
plished as Dodds, Ory, and St. Cyr, they *were* members of
his working band and willing to take his unorthodox instructions. Singleton, on the other hand, was an excellent drummer, and Hines, of course, was a revelation—the first pianist
to play skittery linear figures, reflecting Louis's influence (it
was said of Hines that he played "trumpet-style" piano,
though his attack was orchestral). Hines's unerring sense of
time enabled him to track Armstrong through his most daring conceits.

One of the new Hot 5's records came to symbolize more
than any other the ascendancy of a classic American music.
The most celebrated and analyzed of Armstrong recordings,
"West End Blues" opens with a clarion call to arms—a blaz-
ing virtuoso trumpet cadenza that, in Gunther Schuller's
words, "served notice that jazz had the potential to compete
with the highest order of previously known expression." Its
keening momentum, which defies notation, remains
undimmed and peerless. How can one explain the large
number of violinists who can play Bach's D-minor Cha-

conne when no trumpeter, in or out of jazz, has convincingly replicated Armstrong's nine-measure intro? Working with a strangely banal King Oliver blues, Armstrong refashioned the twelve-bar theme into a sensationally varied performance. Each chorus differs from its neighbors: a sober trombone solo squired by woodblocks; a simple but enchanting duet by clarinet and voice; a dreamy piano solo; and finally, Armstrong's splendent trumpet, holding one perfect note for four measures, then caroming into a pattern of falling arpeggios. The trite clop-cymbal sign-off sounds like an addled expression of amazement.

The recordings of 1928 are widely regarded as Armstrong's peak. The Pittsburgh-born Hines inspired him more than anyone since Oliver, and their collaborations became the foundation for a music utterly independent of the conventions of New Orleans. The greatness of "West End Blues" is undeniable, but it is not an isolated crowning achievement. Armstrong made other records as good that year, and at other junctures in his career. "Muggles" is the foundation for tens of thousands of jazz records that are successions of solos, though few can match its drama. What it lacks in organizational esprit is compensated by a climactic solo in which Armstrong turns a flagging blues into a brisk twenty-four-bar rhythm fantasy plus an emotional twelve-bar blues. His runway is a four-bar break that has as much in common with the preceding solos as a jet has with Wright aircraft. In the next five bars, he bounces between two pitches (A and C) and in the following seven employs only the C and its octave—an imperious example of "less is more." Then he skids into halftime with a four-bar transition, gliding into a closing chorus that is built almost entirely on the expressive power of seventh chords.

"Weather Bird" is the only Armstrong-Hines duet and remains the standard for off-the-cuff encounters. Extreme liberties are taken with the material (a three-strain rag originally recorded by Louis with King Oliver as "Weather Bird Rag") and the meter as the two masters jab and feint in a freely swinging, often witty scuffle that ultimately has them exchanging solitary measures. The competitive edge between the two friends elicits smiles after numerous hearings, but what makes the record most impressive is the unfaltering emotional content. There is beauty in the madness. They go at each other again in an episode of the less compelling "Skip the Gutter." Hines contributes a fanciful backup to Armstrong's vocal on "St. James Infirmary," and plays celeste on the oracular "Basin Street Blues"—a dramatic vignette in which the trumpet emerges *pp* from the hushed ensemble, attains full bloom, and then disappears in favor of a scat vocal that goes deeper than the song's words ever could.

Don Redman, a colleague from the Henderson band, appears on several selections as instrumentalist and composer. His famous "Save It Pretty Mama" offers superb Hines and an Armstrong-style Redman sax solo. "Heah Me Talkin' to Ya?" has supple work by all three, though Armstrong is surprisingly tranquil. Alex Hill's imaginative arrangement of "Beau Koo Jack" features Armstrong's whiplash trumpet breaks. "Tight Like That" is the masterpiece of the Redman sides, engendering one of Louis's most expansive and scrupulous improvisations. The prelude, incorporating risqué vaudeville nonsense, kicks into Armstrong's smoky rendering of the theme and Hines's variations on it. At his return, the trumpeter begins the first of three architectonic choruses with a solemn scene-setting motif (E natural to B natural), played five times. His two subsequent choruses also turn on sturdy motifs (including a naughty ditty from World War I), each opening at a higher interval, so that all three build cumulatively in range and fervor. The subject may be sexual, but the music erects a cathedral of the spirit.

"Tight Like That" manages to be cagey and direct, spare and effusive, vaulting and crude, high and low. In this three-minute spectacle, the entertainer and the artist are inseparable, and bound for trouble among the puritans. What manner of artist spices his performance with rude jokes about pleasures of the flesh? What sort of entertainer can so forthrightly convey the acute sadness of the human comedy? Setting up the final payoff, Armstrong interpolates an adolescent jingle ("Oh, the girls in France . . .") and then makes of that very phrase the stuff of inspired passion. Still, in 1928 Armstrong the entertainer was invariably at the disposal of Armstrong the artist. What would happen if the ebullience behind the artistry were to find shape in sheer personality, unleashed and unfettered?

Part Two

The Artist as Entertainer

One

His brethren could not readily forgive this power of pleasing which, strictly speaking, is a gift. . . . Make no mistake: this is a delightful kind of fame, the secret envy of many of those great purists, who can only warm their hands at the somewhat pallid flame of the approbation of the elect.

—Claude Debussy

DEBUSSY, WRITING AS MONSIEUR CROCHE, was paying homage to a far less innovative musician than Armstrong, Jules Massenet. He admitted that a gift for pleasing "young milliners" was hardly indispensable to art and acknowledged the inhibiting effect of Massenet's fertility. Yet Massenet "was the most truly loved of all contemporary musicians," not because his operas condescended to the public, but because they spoke directly to it—a fact not lost on those who envied his unstoppable success. "To endeavor to overthrow those whom they imitate is the first principle of wisdom with certain artists," Debussy continued, noting that the true artist struggles less with his colleagues than with himself. Like Massenet, Armstrong troubled a core group of his admirers by remaining true to himself rather than to them. He took jazz away from purists, who, it must be said, took an exceedingly long time to claim it but no time at all to promulgate rigid definitions as to its substance, and gave it to the young milliners and anyone else who wanted it.

Armstrong shrugged off the idea that jazz was the private domain of blacks (he was an early supporter of white musicians and led, with Joe Glaser's managerial support, an integrated band, even when it cost him work) or Americans. Urged by the commentator on a 1960 TV show to confirm the common observation that European jazzmen copied Americans, he snapped, "We don't look at it that way. . . . How do we know who copied what?" He understood, as many did not, that the strength of jazz lay in its international appeal and that chauvinistic hauteur implied constraints that were bad for business and for his musical message. By 1960 he was quick to insist that he was an "ambassador" of music only and had nothing to do with politics. Yet his insistence on the universality of jazz was indisputably political, and he put it over with a litany of indisputable maxims. "A note's a note in any language." "Jazz will give you beautiful ideas, make you feel good." "As long as it sounds good, we don't care who wrote it." "The best band in the world is the clowns' band in the circus. You gotta be a good musician to hit a bad note at the right time." "I like trumpet players who play what they feel. If they want a high note, get it over with." "Styles don't faze me." "People love me and my music, and you know I love them. The minute I walk on the bandstand, they know they're going to get something good. I see to that."

Sometimes he responded to interviewers who tried to feed him their own prejudices with the patience of a schoolmarm; sometimes he acquiesced and switched to a lighter subject. At his best, he parried them with wit, as in a 1960 radio interview with British journalists in Kenya. He was questioned about his vices. "I do all the things that you do." About the Noël Coward–like nostalgia of his song "Someday." "Can't you name somebody a little lesser than Noël?" About rock 'n' roll. "Oh, that's our church music." About modern jazz. "They make a thousand notes to get around the one." About his appeal to the young. "Yes, I'm young myself." About his hectic schedule. "I never felt yet that I didn't want to get on that stand." About his popularity in Africa. "Always have been Africans all over New Orleans." About an East African song in his repertory. "We like everything we play." About how high he could go. "Well, I can get up to p." About the duke of Windsor's statement "I'd rather hear Louis Armstrong play 'Tiger Rag' than wander into Westminster Abbey and find the lost chord." "I agree with that."

Those jazz purists who had long since decided Armstrong's place in an arcane schema of the true and false jazz were not amused. In 1946, B. H. Haggin, the bullheaded but sensible music critic for *The Nation*, devoted a column to what he called the "falsifying schematization" of jazz, specifically as it related to Armstrong. A correspondent had written to argue that any critic who failed to distinguish between Armstrong's music of 1925 and his "obviously different music" of 1928 was promoting "hopeless confusion," to which Haggin responded, "The same thing is gained by calling a Hot 5 and a Savoy Ballroom Five both jazz as is gained by calling a work of Mozart and a work of Beethoven both symphony; and confusion is created by giving them two names." By then, Armstrong was very likely the most famous musician in the world and was frequently cited with Charlie Chaplin, Bing Crosby, and Mickey Mouse as the most famous of Americans.

The Armstrong-Hines recordings of 1928 had marked the end of that phase in Armstrong's career when he could confine himself to the province of jazz per se. No longer would a coterie of rapt fans have him to themselves. By 1929, business at the Savoy in Chicago was slow and payments were late. Tommy Rockwell of OKeh Records wired Armstrong to return to New York, offering him work and management. Armstrong showed the wire to Carroll Dickerson, Zutty Singleton, and the others, and they all thought the band was too good to break up. They were living together in a Chicago flat, preparing their own meals, playing poker and blackjack, shooting craps, and being "good sports about it." As Armstrong later wrote Goffin, "I was one guy who always stuck with a bunch of fellows, especially if I liked them." When Rockwell sent a second wire, Armstrong called a meeting of the band.

> I told them, well fellows, you all know how well I love you all, and you boys love me too. What say if we have our cars

fixed up and Mr. Rockwell has just sent me enough money and I can give each man in the band $20 to eat off of and help buy gas, and we'll all go to New York together? They all jumped up into the air with joy and said that's great. . . . We were popular all through the towns we passed through—Toledo, Ohio, Cleveland, Detroit, Buffalo. We went 40 miles out of our way to see Niagara Falls, etc., and everyone was so glad to see us. They all had been hearing our broadcasts from the Savoy Ballroom in Chicago the whole time we were there. . . . Zutty and I were riding in my car. In fact Zutty did pretty near all the driving. I did most of the sleeping . . . and when Zutty arrived in New York, the minute we were crossing 42nd and Broadway my radiator cap blew off and steam was going every place—and were we embarrassed. The cops came over and saw we had Chicago license on our car, and asked us, "Hey there, have you boys any shotguns in that car?" We gladly said, "No suh boss." He smiled and went away. . . . We all finally arrived in Harlem, everybody suffering with the shorts, meaning we were all broke. So I immediately went downtown to Mr. Rockwell's office. He certainly was glad to see me. He said, "Louie" I've just arranged to put you in the *Great Day* show. I said, Oh fine Mr. Rockwell, but, er, wer—I brought my band with me and you'll have to book us someplace. Mr. Rockwell hit the ceiling saying, "Band? I did not send for your band, I sent for you only." I said (very calmly), Just the same Mr. Rockwell, we're here now, I just couldn't leave my boys that's all. I know you can book us someplace. Another thing, we all need money so you'll have to let me have about _____ dollars to keep up eating, room rent, and our laundry until we go to work. After all, they must hold their heads up, and stay sharp because they're all sharp cats and can play their asses off. Finally Mr. Rockwell gave in and gave me all the money I wanted and inside of two weeks we had a job in Connie's Inn in Harlem, at 131st + 7th Ave. That club and the Cotton Club were the hottest clubs in Harlem at that time—and Harlem was really jumping. All the white people would think it was a real treat to spend a night up in Harlem. *(Goffin)*

The incident with the cops and the showdown with Rockwell indicate Armstrong's willingness to play the game when called for and to stand his ground when necessary. His intransigence was as much respected among musicians as his loyalty. One reason he was eventually able to effect what he considered an ideal business partnership and marriage is that he found equally strong and loyal people in Joe Glaser and Lucille Wilson, who knew where he drew the line and respected it. As it turned out, he was lucky to have the band, since he wasn't given a part in *Great Day*, which was a flop anyway. The floor show at Connie's, however, had a score by Fats Waller that attracted enough notice to warrant a shot at Broadway, where it ran 219 performances as *Hot Chocolates*. One of the highlights was Armstrong's rendition of "Ain't Misbehavin'," performed at first from the pit and later onstage. After the show, he'd race back to Connie's Inn in Harlem—"My band really used to play the hell out of Connie's show"—where he'd bring the house down with his backing of Louise Cook's erotic shakedance and lead off the dance set with "Indian Cradle Song." One night the leading white musicians came uptown to Connie's and threw a party for Louis. Bandleader Ben Pollack presented him with a gold watch inscribed, "Good luck always to Louis Armstrong from The Musicians on Broadway."

Of course Louis had had the attention of white jazz players since the time he arrived in Chicago, and as soon as he returned to New York, Eddie Condon convinced Rockwell to let him produce an integrated record date. At 8 A.M. the next morning, Louis was in a recording studio for the first time since "Tight Like That," three months earlier, fronting a mixed band including the marvelous trombonist Jack Teagarden. They recorded a blues jam, "Knockin' a Jug," which Armstrong dominated as effortlessly as he had "Muggles." That same afternoon he fronted Luis Russell's nine-piece band, with Condon and Lonnie Johnson sitting in, and recorded two landmark sides. "Mahogany Hall Stomp," named after Lulu White's Storyville establishment, captures the New Orleans spirit and offers a vivid glimpse of Armstrong the structuralist: The first of his three muted choruses consists of short electric, rhythmically displaced phrases; the second is one full-moon note held for ten measures; and the last is a five-note riff played six times. The solo, so simple and so effective, became a standard part of the piece whenever he played it. The other number put Armstrong on a new course: "I Can't Give You Anything But Love" was his first pop song in the company of an ensemble (Armstrong's admiration for Guy Lombardo's buttery reeds is much in evidence) that did little more than parade the chords as a scrim, leaving him free to distort, kid, and ultimately alchemize the material. Again, his improvisation became a classic in its own right—Ethel Waters sang it verbatim on her recording of the song.

A new Louis Armstrong seemed to be taking over from the old. To some degree, the newness was an illusion. Armstrong had been playing with big bands throughout his years in Chicago. With Erskine Tate's "symphony" he had enjoyed a taste of stardom and a repertory that ranged from movie accompaniments to pop songs to operatic showstoppers. But now he was out of the pit and on the stage. Now he was sharing the domain of Bert Williams and Bill Robinson. He was facing ever larger and more diverse audiences when he sang, dramatizing the song, making it come alive as a vehicle for the fun and games of his incomparable extemporizations. His utterly original way of putting over a song—of selling it, of keeping the audience enchanted with it—was as instinctive and ingenious as any other aspect of his achievement. He figured out how to make his music part of a larger presentation, the Louis Armstrong Show. Like Bojangles, he offered a unique and prodigious talent; like him, too, he presented that talent as one aspect of a giant, all-encompassing personality that could absorb all the light in the room and shine it right back at the audience. "The minute I walk on the bandstand, they know they're going to get something good. *I see to that.*"

Louis Armstrong never aspired to be a studied virtuoso, who walks to center stage, bows, plays God's music, bows again, and leaves. He demanded a reaction whether he played for dancers or listeners. He thrived on the roar of the crowd, and like a great preacher or blues singer, he knew how to elicit the whoops and cries and moans of pleasure. In

1933, he was filmed in Denmark in a stunningly effective presentation that parodies the "correct" performer. "Good evening, ladies and gentlemen," he says, bowing. "I'm Mr. Armstrong." The glint in his eye is mischievous and dauntless: This guy is *in charge*. He counts off the tempo and transforms "Dinah," a cheap ditty, into a miraculous rhapsody in which his every physical movement—the facial mugging, the savvy footwork, and angle of his trumpet—complements the galvanizing irreverence of his music. "There are no bad songs," he once told an interviewer, much as Van Gogh might have said there are no bad colors. Armstrong was no longer one of the boys in the band: He was a musician, singer, bandleader, comic, dancer, actor. That unique radiance heard in "Potato Head Blues" now coursed through the man himself.

During the performance of "Dinah," he extends a phrase in the song's release with a descending scat arpeggio, delivered with a funny bug-eyed expression that is exactly right for the musical content of the phrase. This is known as mugging, a comic art that Armstrong perfected with a skill equal to Jack Benny's deadpan or Oliver Hardy's slow burn or Cary Grant's second take. Armstrong's mugging is so much a part of his vocal performances that it is impossible for anyone who has seen him to listen to his records without imagining his facial contortions. Even when he delivered himself of a ballad, he had an array of expressions—half smiles, a trembling of the lips, a widening of the eyes, a scrunching of the nose—that fit the notes and underscored the lyric. Mugging was a kind of body English done with the face; it was a way of acting out the music. No one else ever did it as well,

and soon no one else did it at all. He was constantly under
attack for mugging: The barbs were ludicrous (he demeaned
his art by clowning) and patronizing (he was playing the role
of an Uncle Tom). During his initial visit to England, in
1932, he was described as "barbaric" by one intellectual,
who admired his music but didn't think lay persons were
ready for the shock of seeing him in the flesh. Indeed, he
was pelted with tomatoes at one concert. In his astute account of that tour, Chris Goddard observed that Armstrong
"shattered all those restricting elements which European
musical attitudes had grafted on to jazz in order to ensure its
status as 'Art.'" Of course the sensibilities of the masses were
largely won over by then, at least in the United States,
though intellectuals on both sides of the Atlantic would continue to stew.

Two

THE RECORDING ARMSTRONG MADE of "Ain't Misbehavin'" at his second session in the summer of 1929 was a hit
that confirmed his burgeoning popularity as well as the use
of pop songs as standard source material for jazz interpretation. Along with his other records in that period, it helped
set the stage for the popular acceptance of jazz that would
follow six years later, after Benny Goodman's triumphant
tour of 1935. For the next seventeen years, Armstrong
would be heard almost exclusively with big bands. His voice
mellowed in the thirties, proving to be far more lithe and
pleasing than anyone expected. It matured into a handsome
tenor, full of feeling and humor, offering irresistible contrast
to the ever increasing brilliance of his instrumental technique. But to many it conveyed an abstruse language of
grunts and moans. Even as late as 1936, in his introduction
to Armstrong's book *Swing That Music*, Rudy Vallee—whose
effete voice and style had once been all the rage—felt
obliged to defend the musicality of Armstrong's vocals:

"They often seem to be the result of a chaotic, disorganized mind struggling to express itself, but those who know anything about modern music recognize his perfect command of time spacing, of rhythm, harmony, and pitch and his flawless understanding of the effects he is striving to achieve."

Armstrong's recording of Waller's "Black and Blue," abetted by a sympathetic trombone and reeds that swoon in commiseration, was invoked by Ralph Ellison in the prologue of *Invisible Man*, to send his hero into a sanctified reverie. Dan Morgenstern has pointed out that the song was originally conceived as the lament of a dark-skinned woman who loses her man to a lighter rival: Not until Louis removed the verse and sang it with "such dignity and passion" did it become "the 'protest' song which from then on it was considered to always have been." Armstrong's two versions of "When You're Smiling," one with a vocal and one without, show the influence of B. A. Rolfe, the star trumpet player with Vincent Lopez's dance band, who prompted him to phrase an octave above the orchestra. Both versions close with rapturous high-note choruses, pure distillations of melody, from which a listener would be hard put to imagine the physical drama that accompanied such music in concert. Fortunately, we have Irving Kolodin's eyewitness account of 1933:

> He announces "When You're Smiling" and this time he has
> a new act. He backs off, downstage left, leans half-way over
> like a quartermiler, begins to count, (swaying as he does)
> "one, two, three" . . . he has already started racing toward
> the rear where the orchestra is ranged, and he hits four, exe-

cutes a slide and a pirouette; winds up facing the audience
and blowing the first note as the orchestra swings into the
tune. It's mad, it's meaningless, it's hokum of the first order,
but the effect is electrifying. No shabby pretenses about
this boy! He knows what his audience will take to their
hearts, and how he gives it to them. His trumpet virtuosity is
endless—triplets, chromatic accented eerie counterpoints
that turn the tune inside out, wild sorties into the giddy
stratosphere where his tone sounds like a dozen flutes in unison, all executed with impeccable style and finish, exploits
that make his contemporaries sound like so many Salvation
Army cornetists. Alternately singing choruses and daubing
with the handkerchief at throat, face, forehead (he perspires
like a dying gladiator) the while a diamond bracelet twinkles
from his wrist, he finally gets off the stage to rest.

In 1930, Armstrong made his first trip to California,
where he was booked into Frank Sebastian's Cotton Club in
Culver City. By that time Tommy Rockwell had been promoting him as a single, which meant a final break with Carroll Dickerson and the men from Chicago. Armstrong later
complained that the breakup was fueled when members of
the band started arriving late for the engagement at Connie's Inn. For one reason or another, management fired him.
But he must have realized, too, that he could no longer
shoulder the responsibility for keeping an orchestra working, and he acquiesced when Rockwell convinced him to
front other bands. The band Leon Elkins led at Sebastian's
Cotton Club included trombonist Lawrence Brown, later a
major figure in the Ellington orchestra, and drummer Li-

onel Hampton, who, Armstrong recalled, played "some little bells which he kept besides his drums, and he was swinging the hell out of them too." About two months into the seven-month gig, a better band was brought in, directed by Les Hite. Artistically, it was another fertile season. He made his first movie, playing incidental music in an independent feature film called *Ex-Flame*, which no longer exists. Through radio, he quickly became a favorite of the Hollywood community, which began to pack the club. He continued to make astonishing records.

His first record in California was his last as a "sideman," and a ringer in his discography: country singer Jimmie Rodgers's "Blue Yodel No. 9," to which he added aggressive obbligato. The sessions with Elkins produced the razzle-dazzle "I'm a Ding Dong Daddy," in which Louis scats enthusiastically ("I done forgot the words," he explains mid-break) and plays a piping climax that coined the phrase Dizzy Gillespie later reset as "Salt Peanuts." The Hite sessions closed with a grandstanding rival in "Shine," which Armstrong made into a tour de force of self-avowal despite a lyric that embodies racial condescension. In his posthumously published comments on "Shine," Otis Ferguson credited it with "a point and rage and loveliness that have nothing to do with the original intention or the auspices under which it was carried out." After a thousand hearings, he noted, "it is still true and good, moving a person to sadness, pride, etc."

Between those monuments of virtuoso transfiguration, he recorded some of his most enduring ballad performances. "I'm Confessin'" suggests that his immense influence on

Bing Crosby was reciprocated. (Armstrong could be a sly parodist. As John Chilton has pointed out, a touch of Al Jolson is heard in "My Sweet," recorded earlier in 1930.) "Body and Soul," which Louis introduced to the jazz repertory, and "If I Could Be with You" are completely refurbished: The soupy saxes and static rhythms spur Armstrong to ever more outlandish conceits. "Sweethearts on Parade" is more remarkable, since the song is trash—his vocal inflections, including sighs and grunts that trail away from the actual words like shadows, are as expressive as his keening trumpet invention, complete with extrovert breaks that quote "High Society" and reveille. (Lucille Armstrong told me he used to say, "Don't listen to the tune I'm playing, listen to the notes I'm playing.") For "Memories of You," Armstrong pulled a vibraphone from a corner of the studio and persuaded Hampton to record his first solo on the instrument.

Still, the trip to California ended in calamity. Every day Louis drove for thirty minutes or so from his room in Los Angeles to the club in Culver City. After work and during intermission, he would occasionally repair to his car to get high on pot. One night he was sharing a joint with Vic Berton, a white drummer who recorded with Red Nichols and others, when the cops busted them. They spent the night in jail and the next morning were sentenced to six months and a thousand dollars each. Rockwell sent a shady character named Johnny Collins out to California to fix the case; the sentences were suspended, though Armstrong and Berton had to stay in the jail hospital weekday nights for a while. Armstrong never forgot the lesson and publicly declared he would never smoke again. His protestations were

considered hilarious in jazz circles, because Armstrong was a
lifelong connoisseur of marijuana. I interviewed more than a
dozen musicians who said Armstrong introduced them to it.
Most of them shook their heads with laughter at how much
he loved rolling cigar-size joints after leaving the bandstand.
It wasn't just a recreational substance to him but a nostrum
on the order of his favorite physic, Swiss Kriss. He swore by
it and proselytized for it—even wrote a letter to Eisenhower
asking him to make it legal again.

At a time when indiscriminate use of physically addictive
drugs is ravaging the country, marijuana is once again vili-
fied as part of the scourge. I don't want to imply anything
heroic in Armstrong's appetite for it, but it was an important
part of his life, and some find a direct link between it and his
live-and-let-live temperament. He started smoking soon after he arrived in Chicago and used one of his nicknames for
it as the title of an early masterpiece, "Muggles." Usually, he
called it gage. He was in all other respects relatively health
conscious. He drank in moderation (never before a gig) and
smoked Camels, but watched his diet, never used hard
drugs, never popped pills. Each day was planned around the
job, and he kept himself in shape for it. After, though, in his
usually mobbed dressing room or on the bus, he would use
pot to unwind. In the sixties, an interviewer asked him how
he felt about the likelihood that marijuana might be legal-
ized. He said, "That won't help the poor cats they put in
jail."

Other troubles brewed in California. Lil came out to see
him, and he discovered she was having an affair with a man
she said was her masseur. Alpha followed shortly after, and

Louis was now determined to get a divorce. Worse, Collins convinced him that he had cut a deal with Rockwell and was now his manager. En route to New York, Armstrong was booked by Collins into a club in Chicago called the Show-boat. The band, which included Zilner Randolph, Charlie Alexander, Preston Jackson, Tubby Hall, Lester Boone, and John Lindsey, was one of his favorites: "Now there's a band that really deserved a whole lot of credit that they didn't get. They made some of my finest recordings with me." Several well-known bandleaders came down to honor "Louie Arm-strong—all white folks call me Louie." Everything seemed to be going fine, until he realized he was caught in the mid-dle of a managerial war with mob overtones.

Funny thing how I did not know that Johnny Collins and Rockwell were having [a] feud over my contract. Why and for what I've never found out till this day. All I know is who-ever were the gang in New York sent gangsters to Chicago where I was working and tried their damndest to frighten me into quitting the job and come to New York to open up back at Connie's Inn again. And I felt that as dirty as Connie fired me and my band, I did not want any parts of those people ever again. I am just that way. If you kick my ass once you can bet I won't go back if I can help it so you can kick it again. And Connie's Inn was going down by degrees, and at that time I was the rage of the nation. But nay nay, never no Connie's Inn. One night the gangsters started a fight in the Showboat in Chicago, right in front of where I was standing playing my trumpet. I usually stood playing with my eyes closed [leaning against a post] down on the dance floor. I mean they were really fighting worse than a bunch of spades. One of the gangsters took a chair and hit a woman over the head with it and the chair crumpled up all in a lot of little pieces. Some of the pieces hit my horn but even *that* could not make me leave the bandstand, you know? The Captain must go down with the ship. Then, too, things like that never frighten me. I've seen too much of that bullshit during my days of playing music. Ain't but one incident at the Showboat that kind of got me, and it happened one night as we were just playing and the people were all dancing and having a ball. Our dressing room was also located on the same side of the bandstand. A pretty large one at that. I usually blow my trumpet with both of my eyes closed and as I was blowing, I felt someone touching me very quietly, speaking in a whisper. It was a big burly-looking gangster saying, "Somebody wants you in the dressing room." I said, "Sure, I'll go in as soon as I finish this dance set." And I didn't pay any attention to it. So after the set was over, I ran real lickety split to my dressing room to see who it was. I rushed to the door thinking it was one of the cats, and there, bless my lamb, who I did see was a white guy with a beard on his face thicker than one of those boys from the House of David. So he spoke first—"Hello" (kind of sarcastically). I still ain't hep to the jive. I said, "Hello" (very pleasantly). He said, "Do you know who I am?" I said, "Why, er, no, no I don't." In fact it really didn't matter as long as he talked about music. I just knew he and I were going to really run our mouths a while musically. Then this guy said, "I am Frankie Foster." At first I still didn't pay any attention—to that extent anyway. Then it dawned on me what he said and I turned in cold sweats. . . . By this time he had his big pistol, pulling it out as he said, "My name is Frankie Foster," and he said he was sent over to my place to see that I catch the first train out to New York. I still try to make it appear that he ain't frightening me. I said, "New York? Why that's news to me. Mr. Collins didn't tell me anything about it." Frankie Foster said, "Oh yes, you're going to New York at Connie's Inn, and you're leaving to-morrow morning." Then he flashed his big ol' pistol and aimed it straight at me. With my eyes as big as saucers and frightened too, I said, "Well, maybe I *am* going to New York." Ooh God. Then Frankie Foster said, "Ok. The tele-phone receiver is down waiting for you to come and say you'll be there. Now you and me are going to the telephone booth and you'll talk." By this time anything he ordered of me was alright, because it is no trouble for a gangster to pull the trigger, especially when they have you cornered and you disobey them. Soooo we went to the phone with a gun in my side and sure enough someone said hello, a familiar voice too. Yes sir, I know that voice if I hear it a hundred years from now. The first words he said to me was, "When are [you] gonna open here?" I turned and looked direct into Frankie Foster's face and said, "Tomorrow. A.M." (*Goffin*)

Armstrong never revealed whose voice he heard on the phone; it may have been Rockwell or Connie Immerman or their gangland sponsor, Owney Madden, who had a distinc-tive voice and was alive and well long after Armstrong wrote Goffin—as was the increasingly powerful Rockwell. In any case, Louis had humored the thugs, but he had no intention of going to New York. Collins managed to sneak him out to Louisville on the eve of the Kentucky Derby, where—even on the run—he managed to make history by leading the first black band ever to play the Roof Garden of the Kentucky Hotel. From there, the band toured the Midwest and the South, including Armstrong's first return to New Orleans, where he played Suburban Gardens—a white nightclub in Jefferson Parish—for three months, visited the Waif's Home, and presided over a baseball team named after him. The boys were so proud of the uniforms, emblazoned with the name ARMSTRONG, and so nervous about tarnishing them, that their playing suffered—much to the chagrin of the team's sponsor. The visit itself was tarnished on the night he opened at Suburban Gardens, when a radio announcer said, "I haven't the heart to announce the nigger on the radio." With the quick-wittedness that made him legendary, Armstrong asked the band for a chord, calmly took the microphone in hand, and did his own introductions. Similarly, when his appearance before a black audience was cancelled without reason, he made sure the black community got word of his promise to make a secret trip to New Orleans to play only for blacks—a vow he kept in 1935, when he slipped into town to play a black dance hall called the Golden Dragon, and was gone before the press ever knew about it.

In the fall of 1931, the band passed through Chicago again, to record. Although Armstrong avoided playing New York and Chicago for most of the next four years, his discography does not indicate much of a disruption in his career because the records he made that year were, as he said, among his best. "Sleepytime Down South" would soon become his theme song. "(I'll Be Glad When You're Dead) You Rascal You" also became an Armstrong trademark, especially after it was reprised the following year in a Betty Boop cartoon in which his disembodied head wails it at a fleeing white figure. Armstrong said that at a 1932 concert in England, he dedicated it to George V with the words, "This one's for you, Rex." It's a motley group we hear on those Chicago sessions, a comedown from the spit-and-polish band on the West Coast, but Louis is a blithe spirit, whether he's crooning "When Your Lover Has Gone" or scaling peak after peak on "Chinatown," the latter a vaudeville tune that—like so much other unlikely material—would become a jazz standard after Louis showed everyone how to make it work. His glissando-break on "Lazy River," following a whirlwind double-time vocal, is so precipitous that skeptical musicians accused him of using a slide trumpet.

His variations on "Between the Devil and the Deep Blue Sea" are neat and modern, as economical as the earlier "Mahogany Hall Stomp": He shapes the first sixteen bars with winding, asymmetrical phrases; uses two sustained high notes for the release; parades a riff to finish the chorus. "Blue Again," with its impeccable phrasing and weighted momentum, is the record Gil Evans said inspired him to become a musician. "I Surrender, Dear," which Rudy Vallee called his "recorded masterpiece," is one of the grandest examples of his vocal art, a glossary of expressive tricks. (You can project Louis Prima's whole career from this performance.) Perhaps the definitive vocal from these sessions is "All of Me," yet another jazz standard introduced by

Armstrong—according to Whitburn's statistics, it would have been number 1 in February 1932, if *Billboard* rankings had existed back then. It's a sublime demonstration of a style that gives the illusion of self-accompaniment. His interpolations, wordless or not (he gets the same mileage from "mmmf" as he does from "oh baby"), extend and answer the vocal line encompassed by the lyrics proper.

When he returned to New York, Armstrong was hit with a lawsuit by Rockwell and Immerman. He countersued, and when an offer came to tour England for the first time, he and Collins jumped at it. Though Armstrong wasn't universally adored on that first venture abroad, the trip was as much a revelation to him as it was to English jazz musicians. Surely he saw his potential for conquering the international arena. Yet his career remained blighted for another two years as his legal predicament obscured his increasing mastery of the stage. Prohibition had come to an end and, with it, some of the control the gangsters exercised over the lives of musicians who worked their gin mills. Still, they continued to turn up the pressure. Louis returned to New York to briefly appear in another Connie Immerman show, *Hot Chocolates of 1932*, and cut a new series of records for Victor, his first label affiliation since OKeh.

The backup bands, though often stiff and encumbered by poor arrangements, included some of the young lions who, having built on Armstrong's foundation, would help to bring the swing era into flower: drummers Chick Webb and Sid Catlett, tenor saxophonist Budd Johnson, pianist Teddy Wilson, and, ironically, an altoist named Louis Jordan, who would challenge Armstrong's preeminence among blacks twenty years later as the leading light of rhythm and blues. The records are uneven, and Louis sometimes seems to strain to compensate for the material. Yet even by the standards he'd already set, and despite his troubled private life and the fitfulness of the band, "I Gotta Right to Sing the Blues" suggested a new peak in his ability to transform a pop song into a far deeper experience. Of course, Harold Arlen's song had a life of its own. No one but Armstrong could have made "That's My Home" or "He's a Son of the South" a compelling experience. A new version of "Basin Street Blues," though it lacked the mystery of the original, dazzled with its offhanded bravura, and the incomparable "Laughin' Louie" confirmed the unpredictability and taste for paradox of a man who was down but a long way from out.

He was soon touring again, returning to Europe the following summer for a long stay—first London, then Scandinavia (a crowd of ten thousand greeted him at the railway station in Denmark), Holland, Belgium, Paris (where he spent a long vacation), Italy, and Switzerland. Early in the tour he broke with Collins, whose heavy drinking, incompetence, and rudeness to the artist he was bleeding had become intolerable. Armstrong remained a wanderer, though. Except for a single session in Paris (which produced the two-part "Sunny Side of the Street," an instrumental ode to pot called "Song of the Vipers," and the pyrotechnics of "Super Tiger Rag"), two and a half years would pass before he made another record.

Three

Louis Armstrong's professional and private lives were at ebb tide when he returned to the United States in 1935. His lip had become infected in Paris and a doctor told him not to play for six months. Collins was suing him for breach of contract. Lil was pressing for divorce, and Alpha, for marriage. He returned to Chicago and renewed his friendship with Joe Glaser, the tough-talking erstwhile manager of the old Sunset Cafe, who was also down on his luck. They formed a partnership that became the most important professional relationship in both of their lives. They didn't socialize much, but they talked on the phone incessantly, and a kind of love developed between them.

Armstrong's devotion to Glaser galled many of his admirers, who were put off by Glaser's crude manners and strong-arm business tactics. He was apparently connected to the mob, at least in his early years, and was rumored to have been involved in a murder. He made himself a millionaire through Armstrong, but then he made Armstrong a millionaire, too. The most frequent criticism of him is that he worked Armstrong and his band too hard, though it's difficult to imagine Louis *not* wanting to work. Even when he was dying, he made notes to himself about returning to the road. It's certainly true, however, that as late as the "Hello, Dolly!" years, Armstrong was playing zigzag one-nighters, traveling in a bus that had no heat (the stylish pianist Billy Kyle is said to have died from pneumonia because of one of those tours). Sallie Young, Trummy Young's widow, recalls that since Louis never complained, the younger musicians didn't feel they had the right to, either. On the other hand, Glaser was probably the only man who could have extricated Armstrong from his managerial war and pushed him to the unprecedented prominence he would soon enjoy. Glaser was notorious for signing potential Armstrong rivals and putting a freeze on their careers. Louis always came first. Jack Bradley recalls that the one time he made a disparaging remark about Glaser in Louis's presence, he was brought to tears by Armstrong's nonstop barrage of curses. He later explained to Bradley, "First there's music, then there's Mr. Glaser, then Lucille."

There is much speculation about how much of Armstrong's earnings Glaser took. Lucille said it was 50 percent, but pointed out that Louis wanted for nothing. Glaser provided the ideal kind of management for him, leaving him free to concentrate on music. He didn't have to worry about taxes, bank accounts, checkbooks, contracts, the hiring or firing of musicians, or anything else but playing. In collusion with Lucille, Glaser once prepared to surprise Louis with an estate on Long Island, but he refused to move from Corona.

He said he liked the neighborhood and the people. He insisted on having two wads of paper money in his pocket every night after the show. One was his, and the other was to dole out to people who lined up for handouts. At an engagement in Los Angeles, an old connection from the Cotton Club days told Louis he was working as a driver but that his car was in the shop and he couldn't pay the bill. Armstrong bought him a limousine. Glaser hit the roof, but he paid for it. It has been argued that Armstrong's insistence on calling him Mr. Glaser when a third party was present indicated some sort of servility. No one says that of Duke Snider, who throughout his autobiography refers to Mr. Rickey. Armstrong was proud of his association with Glaser. When the two disagreed and Louis was adamant, Glaser backed off. A running argument between them concerned pot. According to Jack Bradley, "Glaser would scream and Louis would say, 'Fuck you.'"

Glaser may have reminded Armstrong of the no-nonsense bosses he had known and admired in his honky-tonk days, not to mention the Karnofsky family. Pianist Barbara Carroll, whose husband, Burt Block, worked for Glaser for fifteen years, described him as "very opinionated, very quick to anger, very amusing, though he didn't know he was amusing, and very generous in certain ways. He had tremendous affection for Louis and did whatever he thought would further his career, and from Louis's point of view, what could have been better? He took care of whatever made Louis happy, he was there for him." Something of an eccentric, he kept salamis hanging on the walls of his apartment, drying out, and if he liked you he'd give you one. He was famously crude: He'd order a bowl of peanuts in a posh club and flick the shells on the floor. He employed few men, but his Associated Booking Corp. handled everyone, including Duke Ellington, Dinah Washington, and Billie Holiday. "He was very concerned about Billie," Carroll recalled, "but Louis was his baby." The publicity books he prepared for Louis were fifty-page "manuals" that advise how and in what size typeface he was to be billed. The 1949 edition suggests: "Louis 'Satchmo' Armstrong, world's highest paid colored musician, trumpet player extraordinary and now acclaimed as the international 'Trumpet King of Swing.'"

In a letter to attorney William Hassan, in 1961, Glaser boasts—in a record-breaking run-on—of having brought Louis to Chicago from New Orleans, "when King Oliver was working for me in one of my places and told me to bring up this sensational young trumpet player who he said was even better than King Oliver and of course history shows that Louis Armstrong did prove to be greater and attained greater stardom than King Oliver within a few years." Glaser had little to do with Armstrong's career before 1935, but—according to Armstrong's account—he did put his name in lights for the first time, at the Sunset in 1926. "He watched over Louis like the treasure he was," Duke Ellington wrote. There can be no doubt that however ambivalent anyone else was, Armstrong had very strong feelings about Glaser. On March 31, 1969, lying in bed in Beth Israel Medical Center, Armstrong interrupted a rewrite of his account of the Karnofsky family to write the dedication page of his autobiography:

I dedicate this book
to my manager and pal
Mr. Joe Glaser
The best friend
That I've ever had,
May the Lord Bless him
Watch over him always
His boy and disciple who loved him
dearly. Louis
        Satchmo
            Armstrong

Glaser died two months later, on June 6. On July 29, in a letter to blues singer Little Brother Montgomery, Armstrong
wrote, "I was a sick ass, yea. My manager + my God Joe
Glaser was sick at the same time and it was a toss-up between us who would cut out first. Man it broke my heart
that it was him. I love that man, which the world already
knows. I prayed, as sick as I was, that he would make it. God
bless his soul. He was the greatest for me + all the spades
that he handled."

From the time they shook hands in 1935 (Armstrong told
friends that there was never a written agreement with
Glaser), Louis's star soared. That fall he signed a contract
with Jack Kapp's Decca Records that lasted seven years—
until the recording ban of 1942—and produced some of his
best and certainly his most diverse work. After the ban, Armstrong emerged as one of the industry's few free agents,
recording for RCA, Decca, Columbia, and anyone else who

could afford Glaser's asking price. In 1936, he was featured in a major Paramount film, *Pennies from Heaven,* opposite its producer, Bing Crosby. In 1937, he appeared in two more movies (there would be twenty-eight others during the next thirty-two years), and became the first black performer with a network radio series, sponsored by Fleischmann's Yeast. During the next ten years he became a fixture of the entertainment world. He played the best theaters, dance halls, and nightclubs; kibitzed with Crosby on radio; and recorded a series of unique and inimitable trumpet concertos. Still, he pushed himself, trying to impress other musicians, playing outrageous strings of high notes that would result in a bloodied lip and bring cheers from the crowd and accusations of vulgarity from the critics. He was mesmerized by the spotlight but never unnerved by it. Jean Bach has recalled the night at the Apollo when he was emcee and was supposed to introduce a white adagio team, whose name he could never remember. "So he was announcing the band members, the various acts, and now it came time to announce the adagio number and he said, 'And now folks,' and you can see he's troubled and stalling and he's thinking what the hell are their names, 'cause he knew all the other acts personally. Finally he looks out in desperation and says, *'The two ofays!'*"

Jack Kapp's recording philosophy was to hurl every kind of song at his artists and then hurl the artists at each other. In short order, Armstrong recorded Hawaiian songs, jazz originals, pop tunes, country and western, novelties, spirituals, the Elder Eatmore monologues, as well as encounters with Ella Fitzgerald (the exquisite "You Won't Be Satisfied"), the Mills Brothers, Billie Holiday, Bing Crosby, Gary

Crosby, and the Lynn Murray Choir. Often the material was beneath him, but it didn't much matter. Nearly every session produced at least one gem. Never had his voice sounded quite so appealing as on such records as "Thanks a Million," "Ev'ntide," "You Are My Lucky Star," "I'm Putting All My Eggs in One Basket," and "I Double Dare You," among many others. His trumpet playing entered a phase of fat-toned solos forever arching upward and brought a new generation of players under his spell. Asked what a musician needed on the road, Bunny Berigan quipped, "A toothbrush and a picture of Louis Armstrong."

Armstrong could now make a melody his own simply by virtue of his phrasing. His solos could no longer be evaluated in terms of the distance he placed between the original material and his variations. He had learned how to stare the material down and—through an alchemical combination of rhythmic finesse, unflagging radiance of tone, and perfect taste—turn trite ditties into powerhouse statements. Armstrong the entertainer was recalling King Oliver's dictum to play the melody; Armstrong the artist was seeing that the melody was somehow made worthy of him. Thus a minor effort by Hoagy Carmichael, "Jubilee," became a euphoric march, an extravagant display of brassy richness, in which Louis wails like a second-line king against the strutting trombones in the last chorus. "Skeleton in the Closet," the novelty number from *Pennies from Heaven*, starts with Louis narrating a ghost story (reminding us how winning an actor he was), then suddenly swinging the lyric, and finally transferring it to the trumpet with a soaring two-bar lick that would crop up nearly twenty years later in his "Hello, Dolly!"

solo. With original material, he could be empyrean from the first note: In "Swing That Music" and the swing arrangements of his "Struttin' with Some Barbecue" and Jelly Roll Morton's "Wolverine Blues," his solos journey from inspired exposition through mild embellishment and rhythmic displacement to punching high-note climaxes.

There were other triumphs. In 1938, Armstrong recorded the first jazz version of a spiritual, "When the Saints Go Marching In." The piece, which Edward Boatner had collected and published twenty-two years earlier, had been recorded once by a gospel group but was not widely known. Danny Barker remembered how Mama Lucy criticized her brother for tarting up a piece from the church. When Barker told Armstrong what she had said, he got angry and remarked that she didn't see anything wrong with playing bingo in the church. At one of several 1940 sessions floated by Sid Catlett's drumming, Armstrong chanted three numbers that may constitute the first examples of rap music; the best of them, an original called "You've Got Me Voodoo'd," has such memorable rhymes as *potion/emotion*, *Venus/between us*, and *Circe/mercy*. Armstrong's wit surfaced in other ways. With the success of "Saints," Kapp had him record several spirituals backed by a white choir. On "Going to Shout All over God's Heaven," Louis made known his impatience with writers and choirmasters who put "colored" pronunciations in the mouths of black performers. Armstrong's New Orleans accent was strangely Brooklynesque: He said *woik* and *hoit*. He never said *daid, gwine, see-gar,* or *hebbin*. On "Going to Shout" the white choir intones, "hebbin, hebbin"; Armstrong growls right back at them, "heaven, heaven."

The impressive band that backs Armstrong on the best of his Decca recordings was organized by the Panamanian pianist Luis Russell. In 1919, at seventeen, Russell won a lottery and used his winnings to move to New Orleans. Years later he worked with King Oliver, and ultimately formed his first important band by raiding Oliver of several disgruntled musicians. Russell made a number of excellent records, honing a unique style that combined the buoyant second-line pulse of New Orleans with arrangements and soloists that embodied the best in swing. It was Glaser's brainstorm to sign the Russell band as a touring unit for Louis. Uneven arrangements (by Chappie Willet and Joe Garland) and lack of rehearsal time (the band would often arrive at the studio dog tired from a road tour) combined to keep the pressure on Louis; he had to make the records lively. But the band had a lot going for it, not least a vital rhythm section (Pops Foster on bass and either Sid Catlett or Paul Barbarin on drums) and several fine soloists, including trombonist J. C. Higginbotham, altoist Charlie Holmes, and clarinetists Bingie Madison and Albert Nicholas. Ironically, the greatest figure in the Russell band became odd man out when Louis fronted it; under the circumstances, there was little for Henry Red Allen, a superbly idiosyncratic trumpet player from Algiers, Louisiana, to do. Writing in the hospital in June 1970, Armstrong expressed warm feelings for Russell ("that good New Orleans piano, very tasty and swingy"), Allen, Higginbotham, and the others. "There were several boys from my hometown, N.O., so you can imagine how well I felt at home with them . . . I was very proud and happy to have played in the band every night." He was especially pleased in 1938, when Glaser booked him and the band alongside the Bill Bojangles Robinson Revue at the Cotton Club in downtown New York—not least because it gave him the opportunity to meet a curvy dark-skinned chorine with liquid eyes and a ready smile.

It seemed to me that Lucille was the ideal girl for me. In fact our lives were practically the same. Good common sense—great observers (not for any particular reason), but were not particular about showy people etc. What we didn't have we did without. . . . I paid strict attention to her when she was working in the chorus at the Cotton Club. Beside the salary that she was making at the club there wasn't too much. (Nothing like the girls made that were working for Ziegfeld and his Follies.) With her salary she had to help to take care of her family, which consisted of her mother, her two brothers, Jackie + Sonny, and a sister Janet. . . . For extra money, Lucille had to sell cookies to the members of the cast, which took in everybody, including Bill Robinson and me. Every night before the 1st show Lucille would be a very busy young girl trying to get dressed and put on her 1st show, and get rid of the cookies, which she would bring down from Harlem. . . . One night when Lucille came into my dressing room to deliver my box of cookies, I asked, "Honey? How many boxes do you bring down here every night?" And when she told me, I said to her, "When you come down here with your bundle of cookies, from now on just bring them all in here (meaning my dressing room). I'll take all of them." She did, which took a big load off her mind. I put them aside and when we'd finish work at the club, me and my good man Friday, Bob Smiley, would take them uptown in Harlem and the next day we'd take them over to the school and divide them up among the school kids. They loved them. I did too.

One night when Lucille came into my dressing [room] to deliver her cookies, I just couldn't hold back the deep feeling and the warmth that I had accumulated for her ever since I first laid eyes on her in the front line on the Cotton Club floor . . . swinging in that front line every night, looking beautifuller 'n' beautifuller every night direct in front of me, standing there directing the band and blowing my solos on my trumpet whenever it was time for me to blow 'n' wail. All of those beautiful notes along with Lucille's perfect dancing. Me diggin' those cute little buns of hers. Hmmm. That's when I automatically said to her, "Look, Brown Sugar" (the name that we show folks and musicians gave her during her early days right out the dancing school into show business; I always thought that it was a cute name). I said to Lucille, "You must have at least an inkling." Huh. Lucille raised her big fine eyes at me as if to say, "My, my, where did he get that word." Of course she didn't say it but I could tell by the tone of her eyes that she was wondering like hell. Pretty smart chick to be so young and around us old timers, too. She's *too much*. And to me, she's everything. I said, "Lucille, I might as well tell you right now, I have eyes for you, and have been having them for a long time. And if any of these cats in the show shooting at you, I want to be in the running." Lucille looked at me and just laughed. But before we both knew it, we were taking in the shows (movies) between our shows. Riding uptown in Harlem every night af-

ter our last show. That's when I had that big long rust-
colored Packard car that Mr. Glaser had bought for me, and
boy was it sharp. It was the hottest car in town, and the talk
of the town. Bob Smiley, my right hand man, a tall good-
looking six foot brownskin cat, used to drive this fine long
Packard while Lucille + I would sit in the backseat and she
looking just like a li'l ol' doll and me sharp as a wedding
(you know what) and happier than 2 peas in a pot (pod to
you). (*Archive*).

It remained for Armstrong to divorce Alpha and convince
Lucille of the benefits of Swiss Kriss (he noted they were
both losing their figures from the excess of Italian food they
consumed after their shows). On October 12, 1942, they
married.

Four

IN THE SPRING OF 1943, LUCILLE bought a house in Corona, Queens, a black suburban community about twenty minutes outside of Manhattan. Louis was traveling at the time and expressed vigorous opposition to the idea. America's most famous musician had never owned a house. For more than twenty years, he had lived in hotels and flats, often boarding with black families on the road, living much of his life on buses and trains. Perhaps the fixity of a house frightened him, or the responsibility that went along with it. When he arrived at Penn Station, he took a cab to Harlem to hang out for a few hours before calling home. He asked Lucille to wait outside, told her if he didn't like what he saw, he'd leave. When his cab pulled up, he tipped the driver twenty dollars and asked him to wait. He got out, looked around, saw that Lucille wasn't outside, and finally rang the bell. Lucille opened the door: "Welcome home, honey." "This is our home?" "Yes." He walked around, climbed the stairs to the second floor, where the master bedroom and his office were, went up to the attic, then down to the basement, and out to the yard. She had fixed up every room and prepared an elaborate meal. Louis was speechless. He ran out to the cab and invited the driver in for dinner. The three of them ate and drank for three or four hours.

Armstrong came to love the house, though he didn't spend much time in it until the late sixties. The decor reflected Lucille's interests—he was crushed on returning after a long tour to find she had taken down the centerfolds he'd pasted up in his office. In later years, though, it was a valued retreat for him. The first-floor bathroom was the shrine of a man who had grown up near an outhouse. The walls and ceiling were covered with mirrors and the fixtures ornamented with gold. The sunny kitchen and breakfast nook looked out on the yard. Lucille had an enormous dressing room adjacent to the bedroom, and down the hall Louis had a small rectangular office that became his refuge. He spent hours typing at his desk, listening to music, chatting with visitors. Louis had never owned most of his records. With the introduction of tape, he became obsessed with collecting all his performances and transferring them to reels of tape: It would be a permanent archive of his work, he thought. Sometimes he'd play an opera or one of his old records and improvise along with it, taping the result. He designed elaborate boxes for the tapes, pasting up montages of photographs and magazine typeface.

On his return from the hospital in 1969, he compiled a catalogue of his reel-to-reel tape collection that runs to 175 pages. The taped material includes most of his own records; a recorded message he made for his friend, attorney Bill

Hassan; privately recorded concert performances; a Fleischmann's Yeast broadcast; his radio and TV interviews; a
Tallulah Bankhead recitation; talks with Lucille; unaccom-
panied "rehearsals"; records by Edith Piaf, Johnny Ray, Roy
Eldridge, Bix Beiderbecke, Duke Ellington, Harry James,
Joe Bushkin, Thelonious Monk, Art Tatum, Fats Waller,
and numerous others, some introduced with Armstrong's
comments; home duets with Bobby Hackett; a birthday
party with comments from neighbors; a bull session with
Redd Foxx; risqué jokes recorded backstage at the Chicago
Theater; "chops sessions" with Velma Middleton; Jelly Roll
Morton's Library of Congress recordings with Armstrong's
added narration; a conversation with Robert Merrill; his
readings of letters and holiday greetings from fans; many
TV broadcasts; excerpts from operas, including some that
he sang or played along with; radio broadcasts of Crosby,
Jolson, Cantor, and others; Bea Lillie; Jackie Moms Mabley;
Israeli, Arabic, and Italian folk songs; Martin Luther King's
funeral service; Mary Lou Williams's Mass; a program about
the New York Mets; various New Orleans bands; hotel-
room chatter; a 1963 concert by Pete Seeger; Jimmy Owens
leading the Radio Orchestra of Holland; thirty-seven demos
from his *Country and Western* album; a conversation about
pot with Max Jones; the cast album of *Applause;* and on and
on. Unfortunately, Armstrong usually recorded both sides of
the tape at slow speed; worse, the tapes were closeted in the
sweltering basement of the house for so long that some of
them may no longer be salvageable.

In later years, Lucille would try to convince him to move.
With Glaser's help, she located a property with a mansion

and swimming pool, and drove him out to look it over. He couldn't see the point. He liked living near Shea Stadium, though he let it be known that he was dismayed at not being invited to sing the national anthem at a Mets game. He liked the people in the neighborhood. When he and Lucille had a brick facade built on the house, he asked neighbors if they'd like the same—since it wouldn't be right for his house to look too high and mighty—and had the brickwork extended down the length of the block. He loved the kids who sat with him on the stoop or came in to watch westerns on television. "We've both seen three generations grow up on our block," he wrote in 1970. "White + black, and those kids, when they grew up and got married, their children still come around to our house and visit their friends Louis and Lucille. That's how close they feel towards us . . . when I would return home, all of those kids in my block would be standing there right in front of my door, waiting to help me unload my luggage and take it into the house." When he was a teenager in New Orleans, Louis had adopted the retarded son of a cousin and supported him all his life, but he had no children of his own.

Surely the security Lucille provided him helped shelter him from the storms of the 1940s. First, there was the squabble over bebop. The ultimate comments were made not in magazines, but on records. Armstrong recorded an outlandish parody called "The Boppenpoof Song," which was withdrawn by Decca after two weeks because copyright owners of "The Whiffenpoof Song" found it tasteless; and Dizzy Gillespie, who would later call Armstrong's place in music "unimpeachable," recorded an imitation of his "I'm

Confessin'" that even his target thought was pretty funny. By the late 1940s, Armstrong was more troubled by the popularity of rhythm and blues, which seemed to drain away his audiences, especially in black communities, where he had long been king. Before that, he'd been forced to confront the fact that big bands were no longer economically feasible. Glaser tried to get him to break up the band, but Armstrong held out stubbornly for a while, until the quality of the orchestra itself began to diminish. In 1944, when the band's music director was Teddy McRae and tenor saxophonist Dexter Gordon had a chair, the morale was disastrously low. Producer Milt Gabler, formerly of Commodore Records, had come to Decca and was assigned to supervise the band's first session after the two-year recording ban (a strike called by the American Federation of Musicians): None of the three sides was considered good enough to release.

In 1947 everything turned around again. Armstrong had just completed filming an atrocious movie called *New Orleans*, which seemed to suggest that the story of jazz was nothing more than the passing of a native music from black primitives who inhabited Storyville to the white ruling class. (Billie Holiday, playing a maid, got to introduce the song "Do You Know What It Means to Miss New Orleans," though the dialogue called for her to tell her mistress that it was just a blues she made up while dusting.) As ludicrous as it was, it focused a lot of positive attention on jazz, especially on Armstrong—possibly because it represented a backwater against the new music coming to life after World War II. In any case, the time seemed propitious for Armstrong to scale his music down to the size of a New Orleans ensemble. The first test came in February 1947, when Armstrong appeared with a band led by the gifted New Orleans–born clarinetist Edmond Hall at Carnegie Hall. Three months later, on May 17, he led his own all-star band for two shows, at eight and midnight, at Town Hall. It was the kind of triumph that can determine the direction of an artist's career.

Five

LEONARD BERNSTEIN ONCE SUGGESTED that the reason philistines think jazz a "low-class" music (he was writing in 1955) is that "historically *players* of music seem to lack the dignity of *composers* of music." He argued, however, that "the player of jazz is himself the real composer, which gives him a creative, and therefore *more* dignified status." Although the philistines are still among us, Bernstein's argument seems no more pressing today than a discussion on whether separate-but-equal is a sensible approach to race. That fight has been won, even if the victory is not yet reflected in appropriate government subsidies for its most emblematic musical art. Still, Armstrong's life raises a tangential question: How does the creative genius who is a player-composer sustain a career after the initial burst of creativity? If he follows the examples of great performers of classical music, the answer is to carry one's art into associated realms—teaching, musical activism, writing. Armstrong, however, lived only to perform, and developed an entertainment style that allowed him to perform before huge, clamorous audiences all his life. The wonder is not that he made himself a compelling entertainer, but that despite the toll of countless one-nighters, he sustained a vigorous and, yes, dignified level of artistry.

One of the highlights of his 1947 Town Hall concert was a version of Hoagy Carmichael's "Rockin' Chair." He first recorded it in 1929 as a duet with Carmichael, and it became a fixture in his repertory—but the 1947 version is definitive. Essentially, it consists of two duets: a brief instrumental episode in which his trumpet is heard against Bobby Hackett's, and the comic vocal. Hackett, an incomparably lyrical player who idolized Armstrong but had none of his might, plays a series of figures that spur Armstrong's theme statement; the two seem almost to be playing different instruments—or, put another way, if Hackett's sound is fifty watts, Armstrong's is a hundred and fifty. The bulk of the performance is a vocal duet by Armstrong and Jack Teagarden that illustrates a similar contrast. They take turns singing the melody and providing comic responses, though Armstrong gets all the laughs. At one point, Teagarden is about to sing a response and Armstrong rolls over him with a scat break. The audience cracks up, not just because it's funny, but because it imparts a musical frisson. It may be vaudeville, but it's vaudeville on a very high level.

Town Hall showed Armstrong the way to go. Soon he was on the road with a sextet, Louis Armstrong and the All Stars. For several years, it really was a band of stars, with Teagarden, Trummy Young, or Tyree Glenn on trombone, Barney Bigard or Edmond Hall on clarinet, Earl Hines or Billy Kyle on piano, Sid Catlett or Cozy Cole on drums, and Milt Hinton or the young Arvell Shaw on bass. It was the highest-paid jazz combo in the world, and through a series of concert albums—*At Symphony Hall*, *At Pasadena*, *At the Crescendo*—it revitalized mainstream jazz with a style unlike any other. At a time when most small jazz groups played bop, cool jazz, or Dixieland, the All Stars furnished an alternative that was, in Ellington's useful phrase, beyond category. Only the instrumentation suggested New Orleans traditionalism. The extraordinary level of musicianship, the swing rhythms, the diversity of repertory, and the live-and-let-live ambience of a band that allowed each player to do as he liked during his solo feature, not to mention the comedy routines with singer-dancer Velma Middleton, all suggested a genre beyond genres.

As Louis's popularity continued to grow, Glaser did all he could to manufacture a new identity for him: Louis Armstrong, ambassador of goodwill. That role was solidified in 1956, when he went to West Africa. In Accra, he was greeted by more than one hundred thousand people, an unprecedented turnout for which Armstrong had a ready explanation: "After all, my ancestors came from here and I still have African blood in me." At a concert in Ghana, he sang "Black and Blue" and brought tears to the eyes of Kwame Nkrumah, Ghana's future president and dictator, a moment captured in the film of the tour, *Satchmo the Great*. In the meantime, he produced a string of hit records at home: "A Kiss to Build a Dream On," which he introduced in the movie *The Strip*; "Mack the Knife," which helped spur the Kurt Weill revival; "Blueberry Hill," a 1949 record recycled in 1956 in the wake of Fats Domino's success. He was the

token black performer on dozens of TV shows, often appearing with Bing Crosby and Frank Sinatra—his duet with
Sinatra on "Birth of the Blues" (*The Edsel Show*), in which he
broke through Sinatra's reserve as he had once done for Lillie Delk Christian, was a standout. He was a much honored
man. That's why all hell broke loose when he spoke out on
civil rights.

The year 1957, perhaps the longest in Armstrong's life,
got off to an ominous start. In February, he played a concert
in Knoxville, Tennessee, before a segregated audience of
eight thousand whites and one thousand blacks. A stick of
dynamite was hurled at the auditorium from a passing car.
The unruffled Armstrong told the audience, "That's all
right, folks, it's just the phone," averting a panic. The bombing was blamed on the White Citizens Council, which had
protested the use of the building for concerts attended by
both races. Asked if the incident would affect his southern
tour, Armstrong told a reporter, "Man, I'll play anywhere
they'll listen."

A different kind of controversy hit the papers in July,
when he arrived to play the Newport Jazz Festival and was
told a birthday tribute had been planned and he was expected to appear in every segment of a long show, without
rehearsal. Exhausted when he got off the bus at 5 P.M., he
was appalled when told what was expected of him beginning
at 8. "We haven't rehearsed," he argued, "and I'm not going
to go out there and make a fool of myself." He exploded
when a festival official had the temerity to tell him that since
Ella Fitzgerald was on the show, Velma Middleton could
not appear. "I'm playing with my band and my singer and

none of this other shit." Glaser tried to mollify him, but to no avail. At one point, beleaguered by photographers and hangers-on, he walked into the musicians' room wearing nothing but a rag on his head and told everyone to get the hell out of his dressing room. He played his set his way, Ella sang "Happy Birthday," and that was that. But the press was scathing. Recalling that night, Lucille said, "He kept his own counsel and nobody could turn him around."

On September 19, Armstrong was playing Grand Forks, North Dakota, when Governor Faubus of Arkansas barred black children from entering a school. Armstrong was planning a widely noted tour of Russia for the State Department at the time. He told a reporter that night that he would cancel the tour, because "the way they are treating my people in the South, the government can go to hell." He said Eisenhower was "two-faced," had "no guts," and was allowing Faubus—an "uneducated plowboy"—to run the country. When the reporter showed Armstrong his notes from the interview, Louis signed the paper and wrote, "solid." "It's getting almost so bad," he said, "a colored man hasn't got any country." As to the Russian trip: "I'll do it on my own. The people over there ask me what's wrong with my country, what am I supposed to say?"

A furor ensued, including a call from the State Department asking him to reconsider the trip (Benny Goodman ended up making it). The next day while Armstrong was asleep, his road manager, Pierre Tallerie, told reporters Louis "was sorry he spouted off." When Armstrong woke up, he fired Tallerie and told the press, "He's speaking for himself. My people—the Negroes—are not looking for

anything—we just want a square shake. But when I see on
television and read about a crowd in Arkansas spitting on a
little colored girl—I think I have a right to get sore . . . do
you dig me when I still say I have a right to blow my top
over injustice?" The attacks were immediate, vicious, and
lasted more than a year. Lucille recalled, "Of course he was
hurt, but a lot of the people who led in the attacks, like
Adam Clayton Powell and Sammy Davis, Jr., later got on the
bandwagon when it was safe." Interviewed on TV, Davis
said Armstrong did not speak for the Negro people, called
him "a great credit to his race," and finally conceded that he
agreed with his meaning but not "his choice of words."

After Eisenhower sent troops into Arkansas and explained
why on television, Armstrong said, "Things are looking better than before," and sent a wire to the White House: "If
you decide to walk into the schools with the little colored
kids, take me along, Daddy. God bless you." But he put
more fuel on the fire in October, when he remarked that
he'd rather play in the Soviet Union than in Arkansas, because Faubus "might hear a couple of notes—and he don't
deserve that." He was, in fact, scheduled to perform at
Arkansas University, an engagement that was cancelled by
vote of the student body. Glaser responded, "Who cares?"
In January 1958, Jim Bishop, a columnist for the *New York
Journal-American*, called for a boycott of Armstrong's concerts. "He is scheduled to star on an upcoming TV show,"
the author of *The Day Christ Died* wrote. "For one, I will not
look." He concluded, "I checked the newspaper files to see
what Louis Armstrong had done for the people of his race. I
haven't found anything and now I ask the musician himself:

'What have you done for your people, except hurt them?'"
The following May, Armstrong was set to appear on *The Steve Allen Show* along with Van Cliburn. Allen hoped they would play a duet. Cliburn's manager refused, fearing for his client's image, but when the show was over the two musicians played "Melancholy Baby."

On the assumption that all the fuss would have interested the FBI, I requested Armstrong's file under the Freedom of Information Act, and was surprised to discover that the G-men had started tracking him in 1948, when his name appeared in the address book of someone they considered suspect. In 1950, an informer told the FBI that Armstrong was dissatisfied "with the situation" at the Flamingo Hotel, but was assuaged with "a bottle of scotch and a couple of reefers." He came to their attention again in 1951, when his name appeared on the letterhead of the Negro Actors Guild of America, Inc. The file heated up in 1956, when Louis was invited to participate in a "Congress of Scholars of the Negro World" in Paris, sponsored "by the leftist 'Présence Africaine,'" and was solicited by actor-politician George Murphy to play at Eisenhower's Inaugural Ball. The file for 1957 records the Knoxville bombing, Armstrong's press conferences, the cancelled concert in Arkansas, as well as an anonymous letter stating, "Louis 'Satcho' [sic] Armstrong is a communist, why does State Dept. give him a passport?"; a signed letter asserting that he is "a patriotic American"; clippings regarding his 1960 tour of Eastern Europe and Africa, including notification that "a Communist Propaganda Booklet Attacking US Racial Policy" was distributed in Lomé, Togoland, "at approximately the dates on which

Louis Armstrong performed in Lomé"; a comment from J. Edgar Hoover himself on an admiring letter about Armstrong, indicating "that Armstrong's life is a good argument against the theory that Negroes are inferior"; a 1965 document issued by the White House that says Jack Valenti requested a name check on Armstrong; and a 1963 three-page teletype to the Dallas office concerning Jack Ruby's unsuccessful attempt to do business with Joseph Glaser.

Curiously, they had no information on the accusation made by Egyptian authorities in 1959 that Armstrong was the leader of an Israeli espionage network (to which Louis replied, "Why don't you tell these people who are spreading all this stuff to come around and I'll tell them a few good traveling salesmen jokes"); or about the 1964 cancellation of an Armstrong concert by the University of Alabama, and the refusal that same year by South Africa to allow Armstrong to perform there with a mixed band; or about his remarks in Copenhagen in 1965 after he read of the riots in Selma ("They would beat Jesus if he was black and marched"); or his refusal to appear on the Oscar telecast in 1968, after the assassination of Martin Luther King, Jr., an action in which he was joined by Sidney Poitier, Diahann Carroll, and Sammy Davis, Jr.

The criticisms of 1957 took their toll, and the inexplicable accusations of Tomming cut deep. Lucille defended his decision not to march. "He gave money, but there was no point in marching and getting his mouth bashed in. He was an artist first. He talked politics with me and he was aware that every word he said had impact." When Larry King interviewed Armstrong in 1967 for *Harper's*, he said, "As time went on and I made a reputation I had it put in my contracts that I wouldn't *play* no place I couldn't *stay*. I was the first Negro in the business to crack them big white hotels—Oh yeah! I pioneered, Pops! Nobody much remembers that these days." Two years later, writing in his notebook, he elaborated on his resentment:

I think that I have always done great things about uplifting my race, but wasn't appreciated. I am just a musician, and still remember the time, as an American citizen, I spoke up for my people during a big integration riot—Little Rock, remember? I wrote Eisenhower. My first comment, or compliment, whatever you would call it, came from a Negro boy from my hometown New Orleans. The first words that he said to me after reading what I had said in the papers concerning the Little Rock deal—he said as we [were] sitting down at a table to have a drink. He looked straight at me and said, "Nigger, you better stop talking about those white people like you did." Hmmm. I was trying to stop those unnecessary head whippings at the time—that's all. (*Archive*)

If Armstrong had an insatiable appetite for applause, he was imbued with the kind of pride that allowed him to choose his honors with more discrimination than is generally realized. In 1949, when his fame was fanned by the success of the All Stars, he was invited to be king of the Zulus at the New Orleans Mardi Gras. He jumped at the chance and reveled in the ceremony. The press and some musicians attacked him for participating in what they considered a barbaric ritual, because the king must wear blackface. Yet for

Armstrong, the invitation was the equivalent of getting an honorary degree from one's alma mater. Twenty years later, in a year when the White House earned reams of positive publicity for honoring Duke Ellington on his seventieth birthday, the office of Nixon's "cultural adviser," Leonard Garment, called Jack Bradley and said, "The White House is interested in Louis this coming year, can you intercede?" Armstrong's reply: "Fuck that shit. Why didn't they do it before? The only reason he would want me to play there now is to make some niggers happy." Republicans, like elephants, never forget. The week Armstrong died, Rep. Charles Rangel, a Democrat from New York, recommended him for a Medal of Honor. According to Rangel's office, "It wasn't even reported out of committee."

Six

LOUIS ARMSTRONG'S FAME DURING THE FIFTIES and sixties has long obscured his musical achievement in those years. The All Stars concerts fell into a routine, though as Lucille was quick to point out, "He always opened with 'Indiana' and closed with his theme, 'Sleepytime Down South,' but the rest of the program he would change to suit the audience. His mind worked so fast. He could hear gnats walking on cotton." When a new player came into the band, Armstrong let him find his way through the music in his own way. His instructions to Cozy Cole were, "We don't have time to say a lot of things up there, just cock your ear and straight ahead." Arvell Shaw didn't realize he was doing okay until he'd played several gigs and Louis started turning around to him, smiling. Milt Hinton was amazed at how much pressure Armstrong put on himself to play something fresh every night. According to Cole, he "really played" about 80 percent of the time; his chops would be down the other 20. During the height of the All Stars' success, when

"Hello, Dolly!" was riding the charts, a typical concert might go like this:

First a brief strain from "Sleepytime Down South," ending with Armstrong singing—arms outstretched, face crinkled with a grin—"Good evening, everybody." Then the inevitable "Indiana." After one of his signal tunes, perhaps "A Kiss to Build a Dream On," he'd say, "Now we're gonna take you down to my hometown, New Orleans," and play "My Bucket's Got a Hole in It" or "Tiger Rag" or "Way Down Yonder in New Orleans." About this time a sideman would get a feature number, which he was free to choose. Billy Kyle might play "When I Grow Too Old to Dream." Armstrong would be back to lead the band through a rousing "good old good one," like "Perdido." "Hello, Dolly!" would be done with two or three encores—he would give his name differently each time: "Hello, Dolly, this is Louis/Satchmo/Dippermouth"—and he never ran out of new trumpet variations. Now the clarinetist would get the spotlight—Eddie Shu might play "Memories of You"; in earlier days, Barney Bigard would do a flashy "Just You, Just Me." Louis would return for "Ole Miss," another exuberant instrumental. His woman singer's primary responsibility was to give Armstrong and the others a rest. In the sixties, Jewell Brown would get the stage to do two or three numbers, like "Lover, Come Back to Me" and "Can't Help Lovin' Dat Man." In the fifties, he toured and sometimes recorded with Velma Middleton, an undistinguished singer to whom Louis was stubbornly loyal. An overweight woman with a girlish voice and the surprising ability to do splits, she could be a funny foil for him, and their risqué duets on such songs as

"Baby, It's Cold Outside" often brought the house down. Armstrong might close the first set with "The Saints." During the second set, the other musicians would have their specialty numbers. The trombonist would additionally sing a duet or two with Armstrong: Teagarden, Trummy Young, and Tyree Glenn all developed routines with him on "Rockin' Chair" or "That's My Desire" or "Back O' Town Blues." Arvell Shaw's pet number was "How High the Moon," with interpolations of Charlie Parker's "Ornithology." In the early days of the All Stars, Sid Catlett's drum solo was "Mop Mop," which Louis called "our bebop number, the only one in our files." In later years, Danny Barcelona, a journeyman drummer hired as a favor to Trummy Young, would find space for a windy smash-'em-up. Along the way, Louis would sing hits of forty years, like "Blueberry Hill" or "Lazy River" or "La Vie en Rose" or "I'm Confessin'" or "Mack the Knife," as well as his lovely ballad "Someday," which he said came to him (words and music) in a dream during a road tour. You knew the end was near when trombone and clarinet crooned a tender chord and Armstrong sang, "Now the pale moon's shining"—the first words of "Sleepytime."

Not surprisingly, young jazz enthusiasts and many critics no longer attended his performances or bought his records. He was considered old-fashioned by many. Jazz had forged new worlds, and even Armstrong's demeanor seemed suspect in a day when jazz musicians were doing everything they could to avoid the label of entertainer. The point was to be hip and cool, like Miles Davis. Anyone who remembered the ruckus caused by Miles when he played with his back to the audience could only marvel at the pleasure he learned to take in later years as he found his own way to flirt with the audience. Davis himself remained one of Armstrong's most steadfast admirers. Still, jazz musicians were demanding respect as artists, and Armstrong, who was paradoxically the most respected of all jazz musicians, seemed to undermine their cause. He had too much fun out there. It was embarrassing. Artists were not supposed to grin and mug and roll their eyes.

The English music journal *Melody Maker*, though a pioneering advocate of Armstrong's art, felt obliged in 1957 to publish the opinions of one Chris Nelms, who said that Armstrong couldn't really play, that his "bleatings" didn't swing, that he had done nothing for music except line his own pockets. He was incensed that a musician with "the public stature of Louis" would say, when asked onstage by his pianist for a key, "I don't know, man, but it starts on my first valve." They weren't amused in the courts of Münster, Germany, either. It seems Glaser sued for a tax abatement on the grounds that Louis was an artist. According to a newspaper account, German law stipulated, "If it moves, it's entertainment, if it doesn't move, it's art." If it's art, you only have to pay half the regular entertainment tax. A professor from the Münster University of Music testified that Armstrong was indisputably an artist, but witnesses described unlikely movements onstage ("the clarinetist performed cartwheels," one reported) and Armstrong was designated an entertainer.

Armstrong's artistry continued to shine forth on records. While Joe Glaser refused to let him sign an exclusive contract and pushed for hits that would get radio play, a few producers—notably, Milt Gabler at Decca, George Avakian at Columbia, and Norman Granz at Verve—created sympathetic environments that produced outstanding performances and made use of the thematic possibilities inherent in the new long-playing format. Among several splendid albums were tributes to W. C. Handy and Fats Waller. Avakian liked to experiment with tape and he produced some memorable effects, including a seamless splice between vocal and trumpet on an exalted version of Waller's "Blue Turning Gray Over You" and an overdubbed duet on Handy's "Make Me a Pallet on the Floor." Granz presented him in the context of a large orchestra, arranged by Russ Garcia, for a program of sophisticated pop songs and a uniquely autumnal interpretation of *Porgy and Bess*, opposite Ella Fitzgerald. Two albums of duets by Armstrong and Fitzgerald, backed by the Oscar Peterson Quartet, were no less effective. They energized each other on swinging material like "I'm Putting All My Eggs in One Basket"; on ballads ("Tenderly" is an unforgettable example), Armstrong showed he could still tap deep wellsprings.

Perhaps the most satisfying recording project of all was the four-volume retrospective, *Satchmo*, elaborately annotated and boxed, with Armstrong's own narration between numbers. "I said someday they're going to do the life of Louis Armstrong," Gabler recalled, "and they're going to have to go to Columbia for all the OKehs. I thought I better go back and record on good clean tape, so I used Bobby Haggart to do the Hot 5s and 7s and Sy Oliver for the rest, copying the original arrangement. Louis got such a kick out of doing it." At first, Armstrong would come in and record three hours in the afternoon, then have to rush to play a gig that would end at 1 A.M. The musicians were tired and grousing. Gabler convinced Glaser to let him pay whatever he would have made from a nightclub gig in addition to the recording fee, so that the band could record at night and at full capacity. Sy Oliver wrote the trumpet parts in red ink on the lead sheets but wrote under them, "Go for yourself." Armstrong often did, and much of the playing is inspired— for example, "King of the Zulus," a dramatic improvement on the old Hot 5 version.

For a while there *was* talk about a Hollywood biopic—in a letter to Goffin, Armstrong said he wanted Louise Beavers to play his mother—but nothing came of it. Still, he contin- ued to make guest appearances in the terminally dumb pseudojazz flicks of the day. He astonished several people on the set of *The Glenn Miller Story* when James Stewart—who was studying trombone for the lead role—asked him if he had any advice for keeping his lips from getting sore. "Yeah, daddy, when you go home tonight, have your old lady sit on your face." Everyone fell out the next morning when Stew- art arrived on the set, looked at Louis, and gave him a salute. Armstrong could apparently disarm anyone. Two stories of his visit to the Vatican quickly made the rounds in musi- cians' circles. In one, the Pope holds out his ring and Louis slides his palm under it in a "gimme five" gesture. In the other, Pope Paul VI asked him if he had children and Louis said, "No, daddy, but we're still wailing."

Armstrong's wit, his utter lack of pretentiousness, and his unpredictability were legendary. It was on the Tommy

Dorsey show that the bandleader innocently asked him what tempo he preferred and heard, "Not too slow, not too fast, just half-fast." Erroll Garner liked to tell about the time he stuck his head in Louis's dressing room after a show and said, "What's new?" "Nothin' new," came back at him. "White folks still ahead." Bobby Hackett told writer Max Jones of the rehearsal that Armstrong halted when a young trumpet player hit an A natural instead of an A flat. The kid, arrogant and determined to show off, said, "Well, you know, Pop, things change, man. Nothin' ever stays the same." Armstrong walked up to him and said, "Man, I'll tell you one thing that'll never change." "What's that?" "You'll always be a spade. You can bet on that. That ain't gonna *change!*" One year he posed sitting on the toilet in a homemade ad for Swiss Kriss and sent it out as a Christmas card. Jack Bradley, who frequently photographed him backstage, once shot him from behind when he was naked and unaware. He brought a print to Louis a couple of days later and asked if he minded if he kept a copy for himself. "No, daddy," he said. "Print up a thousand, send 'em to everybody." With Lucille's connivance, Bradley once sneaked up on him in a grotesque mask. Armstrong looked up and said, "Oh, hi Jack." When he removed the mask, Louis shrieked in horror. He could surprise his musicians, too. On December 1, 1963, nine days after the killing in Dallas, the All Stars played a concert at Smith College. At the end of the show, as the ensemble was about to go into "Sleepytime," Louis walked to the mike and, unaccompanied, played a dirgelike interpretation of "God Bless America." When he finished, he told the stunned audience,

"That was for President Kennedy. Good night," and left the stage.

He never lost his sense of competition. Armstrong loved Trummy Young, the trombonist and singer who had starred with the Jimmie Lunceford Orchestra in the 1930s; Louis saved his career by buying him a new set of teeth and encouraging him when he'd fallen on hard times, and Trummy eventually became one of the most popular members of the All Stars. Yet one night Trummy upstaged him and Louis told him to lay back. The next night Armstrong took too much Swiss Kriss and needed to leave the stage—"Take over," he told Trummy. "But, Pops, you told me to lay back." Louis just glared at him and no more was said on the subject. He rarely lost his temper, but he could be fierce when he did. Danny Barker once said Louis could get so mad he'd suck all the air out of the room. Lucille said, "I think he invented cuss words, he had some I've never heard before. But his anger was always justified—he didn't hold things in." Bobby Hackett has told of the 1953 tour by Louis and Benny Goodman, which had an advance sale of over $1 million. Goodman told him it was his package and Armstrong would do as he was told. "You're nothin'," Armstrong told him, and proceeded to outplay him so badly that Goodman became sick. In Hackett's words, "Pops came close to killing him without touching him, just playing." Years later, when Jimmie Noone's name came up in an interview, Louis said, "Oh that's where Benny Goodman got his whole style."

By the early 1960s, Armstrong's career was in need of a boost. The Little Rock controversy had taken a lot out of him, and in 1959 he suffered a heart attack while playing in

Spoleto. He often experienced shortness of breath and was instructed not to play the trumpet for periods of time. His latest records were uneven, and several suggested a willingness to embrace the neo-Dixieland revival. Gil Evans met him one night and was amazed that Armstrong knew and admired his collaboration with Miles Davis on *Porgy and Bess*. Armstrong was Evans's god, the man he considered most responsible for inspiring him to become a musician. When Armstrong suggested a collaboration—he jokingly added, "You're not gonna throw any of them funny chords at me, are you, Pops?"—Evans followed up with a visit to Glaser's office. "Gil who?" Glaser wouldn't consider it, and Evans, who never brought it up again, always wondered if Armstrong thought he was the one who lost interest. Louis did make three remarkable records in 1961: Producer Bob Thiele managed to get him together with Duke Ellington for two trenchant albums in which, as usual, the superb musicianship proved mutually rejuvenating—the result is superbly played, modern, and beyond category; and Dave and Iola Brubeck wrote a Broadway-style musical called *The Real Ambassadors*, which, though dated in its topical references, spills over with Armstrong's majestic horn and magnetic voice. What he and Glaser coveted, however, was a record that could get radio play.

In 1963, David Merrick was set to bring a new musical to Broadway and he needed someone to record the title song. Louis was chosen and on December 3, the score's publisher took him to a studio to record "Hello, Dolly!" and another Broadway song, "A Lot of Livin' to Do," from *Bye Bye Birdie*. Armstrong shook his head in dismay when he read

the lead sheet for "Dolly," according to Jack Bradley, who
wrote about the session in a jazz magazine and predicted
that given the right push, "A Lot of Livin' to Do" just might
get some airplay. The two sides were sold to Kapp Records,
and eight weeks later "Hello, Dolly!" was on the *Billboard*
charts, where it remained for twenty-two weeks, reaching
the number 1 spot in May. If you remember 1964, you may
cringe at the mention of "Hello, Dolly!" because it was
ubiquitous. It's possible to hear something too much, and
"Dolly" was on radio day and night, and Armstrong seemed
to be on television almost as much. He made all the talk and
variety shows, and even sang it a capella on *What's My Line?*
Less than two and a half minutes long, "Hello, Dolly!" was a
triumph for him, for his generation, for jazz. It was also a
class record.

One of the classiest things about it was its independence
from the formulas of mainstream pop. True, strings were
added for sweetening, but they are barely audible. The only
real compromise with the standard approach and instrumentation of the All Stars was the addition of a banjo. The trite
song, which has had virtually no life beyond Armstrong and
the show itself, was an unswinging set piece on Broadway,
pompous and logy. Armstrong had transformed dross into
gold once again, and even got to play a full chorus of trumpet. The banjo was an ingenious touch. By the sixties, that
ancient instrument, which dominated nineteenth-century
popular music (whole minstrel troupes played them in unison) was little heard beyond Dixieland and bluegrass. The
eight-bar banjo intro, oddly electric and percussive, worked
like an alarm clock to introduce a performance unlike any-

thing else on the Top Forty. The Dolly whom Armstrong so enthusiastically welcomed back was, as Frank Sinatra (who soon recorded a version he called "Hello, Louis") and others realized, none other than himself—back on top where he belonged. Louis's rhythm section and the backing by Trummy Young and clarinetist Joe Darensbourg were right on the money, and his trumpet solo and burnished vocal were ringingly, inimitably Armstrongian. The whole performance was casually flawless.

Kapp rushed him back into the studio to cut ten more tunes so he could issue an album; predictably, there were attempts to imitate the formula—All Stars + banjo + hokey Broadway song = big bucks. Lacking the spontaneity of the original, they didn't always work (though Louis's trombone-like singing on "Mame" is effervescent). Yet Armstrong's career was on a new course, and though his friends wished he would take it easy, he spent his sixty-third year, and the years that followed, on a bus, weaving from city to city and apparently relishing every gig. When the godawful film of *Hello, Dolly!* was made, David Merrick gave Armstrong the royal treatment and star billing, even though he was only in it for two and a half minutes. It was no secret that his record made the show a megahit, the longest-running Broadway musical up to that time. At screenings of the film, it was not unusual for audiences to applaud only during the climactic moment when the camera pans over to Armstrong and settles, at long last, on his mug—direct sunlight in an otherwise fluorescent movie.

Seven

Louis Armstrong's recorded works span nearly forty-eight years. In that time he employed about twelve hundred musicians in the service of more than a thousand songs, some of which he performed repeatedly in the presence of recording devices: "Sleepytime Down South" (his theme song) ninety-eight times; "When the Saints Go Marching In" fifty-eight times; "Basin Street Blues" fifty-three times; "Indiana" forty-seven times; "Muskrat Ramble" and "Struttin' with Some Barbecue" forty-three times; "Mack the Knife" forty-two times; "St. Louis Blues" forty times. Those figures are drawn from Hans Westerberg's Louis Armstrong discography, which was published in 1981—numerous other performances have come to light since then. Even if one had the room to house all of Armstrong's recordings, legitimate and otherwise, one wouldn't necessarily want to listen to them all.

Yet notwithstanding the many meretricious, trite, foolish, formulaic, repetitive, tired records Armstrong was asked to make, the majority of his recorded performances are rewarding, often surprisingly so. In the late 1960s, for example, when he worked primarily as a singer; he was asked to interpret stage and film songs of the period, as well as country songs, Disney songs, and such "timely" nonsense as "His Father Wore Long Hair," which has something to do with Jesus' father. Hip jazz fans did not buy those records, and they remain virtually unknown. I regret as much as anyone that Armstrong's last visits to the studio were supervised by cornballs, but there are gems—truly—even from those sessions. At the "Long Hair" session, he also suffered the indignity of having to sing "We Shall Overcome" with a chorus of celebrities, as well as "Give Peace a Chance" and the equally dated "The Creator Has a Master Plan" with Leon Thomas. That was his penultimate and probably worst album ever (although the country album that followed is a fair rival). His voice was burned to a husk. Yet his readings of "My One and Only Love," "Mood Indigo," and "What a Wonderful World" are poignant and treasurable, and his asides on the other tracks (e.g., "give me a little ol' peace, de-ah") remind us that he wasn't buying anybody's sentimental jive. You could lead Armstrong to the age of Aquarius, but you couldn't make him hallucinate.

Then there's "I Will Wait for You," the tear-jerking ballad from *The Umbrellas of Cherbourg*. Armstrong's is surely the only version in which the listener is made to understand why he's waiting and what he's got in mind for her when she gets there. His asides are happily lubricious, and one is bound to recall with pleasure that they come from the same man who created "Tight Like That" forty years earlier. For the same album, he was asked to salvage "Talk to the Animals," the song that almost brought Rex Harrison's career to a standstill. While the choir talks to the animals, Louis talks to them. When they mention crocodiles, he interpolates in about half a second, "scared of me as I am of them."

Disney Songs the Satchmo Way, recorded in 1968, contains Louis Armstrong's last great trumpet solos and is a masterpiece of its kind—in some ways the ultimate test of his alchemical powers. It's a record for children—with whistlers, a jolly choir, and arrangements that are square but never as cloying as they could be. Armstrong finds something of his own in every song. Through the kind of careful editing that characterized the Handy and Waller albums, his vocals and solos lead one to the other without a break, and they are spirited and inventive. One is not too surprised that he can find beauty in "When You Wish Upon a Star," though one may be startled at how effective his modalized reading of "Chim Chim Cher-ee" is, especially his two darkly beautiful sixteen-bar trumpet solos. The payoff, though, is the presumably intransigent material, like "Bibbidi-Bobbidi-Boo" (he attacks the nonsense syllables with contagious gusto), "Heigh Ho," "Whistle While You Work," and, most surprisingly, "The Ballad of Davy Crockett," which he interprets with a witty storyteller's parlando ("Oh, the buckskin buccaneer," he chortles as though he were having the time of his life), then lifts his trumpet to wail twenty-four bars in perfect hoedown rhythm. His performances here are the work of a great actor, and of an artist of incomparable naturalness and generosity.

He must have been in much discomfort during the Disney sessions. The purity of his sound on trumpet, especially, is all the more miraculous considering the state of his health. The arteries in his legs were clotted, which contributed to his heart problem, and he was habitually out of breath. He suffered from ulcers and kidney problems. Still, he went from Disneyland to London, then back to Las Vegas, before submitting himself to hospital care in late 1968. In early 1969, he had to undergo a tracheotomy, and it was during his recuperation in Beth Israel that he learned of Joe Glaser's fatal stroke and insisted on seeing him, though he lay in a coma. When Armstrong was allowed home, he wrote furiously, digging into the deep past and paying tribute to the doctors and nurses who cared for him. He went back to London twice, recording the theme song to the James Bond movie *On Her Majesty's Secret Service* in 1969, and during the following year appeared on more than a dozen television shows in New York and Los Angeles. For *Esquire's* December 1969 issue, he was one of several artists at or nearing seventy who were invited to offer advice to the next generation. "I feel that I did my interesting work as I have gotten into the older age bracket," he wrote. "Most of your great composers—musicians—are elderly people, way up there in age—they will live forever. There's no such thing as on the way out. As long as you are still doing something interesting and good. You are in business as long as you are breathing. Yeah."

Louis celebrated his official seventieth birthday at the Newport Jazz Festival in June. The Eureka Jazz Band, half a dozen trumpet stars, including Dizzy Gillespie and Bobby

Hackett, and Mahalia Jackson were on hand to pay him homage. A furious downpour started shortly before he was scheduled to go on, and he walked out early so people wouldn't have to wait in the rain. It was customary during downpours for people to run back to the food kiosks for shelter or to hoist tarpaulins. On that evening, they stayed put, cheering in the rain, while Louis romped medley-fashion through several of his hits, assuring everyone from time to time that he wouldn't keep them long. Another party ensued in Hollywood. Two weeks before Newport, he had started to compose a letter to his fans. Reproduced here in its entirety, it begins "This is Louis Satchmo Armstrong speaking from his home in Corona":

I've just gotten out of the Beth Israel Hospital. I've had a million things that happened to me, including the operation for tracheotomy. And I'm coming along just fine and I'm getting my strength back, even in my legs, I thought that it is real thrilling to send a message to my fans and friends from all over the world. Which I'd like to thank all of them from every nook and corner of the world, for their lovely get well cards and prayers which did wonders for me. I also want to thank my personal Doctor Gary Zucker—his staff of doctors, Mrs. Lucille Armstrong, Dr. Alexander Schiff, our company doctor, Ira Mangel, our road manager for many years for many years [sic], and still is. That is if I ever get back to work again. I am looking forward to it. I feel that I owe them, my public and fans, my services again. Which they are eagerly waiting for. I would also like all the nurses in intensive care [sic]—God bless them all. They worked so very hard along with my Dr. Zucker to save my life. And God knows that I was in real bad shape. I also would like to thank the private nurses on the 11th floor of the Beth Israel Hospital who served me around the clock. They were all so nice and kind. (*Archive*)

He accepted an ill-advised engagement at New York's Waldorf-Astoria early in 1971 (he performed most of the time sitting down), followed by a couple of television guest shots. On February 26, in his home, he made his last record, an energetic reading of "The Night Before Christmas," later distributed as a single by the Lorillard Company. He had another heart attack two weeks later and was put in intensive care until May 5, when he insisted on going home. On July 5, he asked Dr. Schiff to bring the band together for a rehearsal—he was ready to perform again. He passed away at five-thirty the next morning.

Appendix

In this document, presumably written in 1968, though it may have been later, Louis Armstrong copied out a letter from a childhood friend, interpolating his own comments. Their voices merge in a catalogue of names (and what names!) from their childhood days in New Orleans. I've attempted to distinguish Armstrong's observations from those of Larry Amadee, his correspondent, by printing the latter in italics; much guesswork was involved in that, especially since both men refer to Armstrong in the third person. I've maintained the style almost exactly, except for Armstrong's tendency to arbitrarily—or so it seems to me—capitalize and underline words. I've checked and corrected spellings of proper names where possible. One or two addresses of dance halls may be wrong, but Armstrong's memory is basically reliable. At the very end, Armstrong wrote "'s all," then crossed it out and wrote "more," adding the note about Fate Marable's opening theme. Of special interest are the new details concerning Armstrong's arrival in Chicago. Generally, his memory in 1968 bears out his recollections of 1954, in *Satchmo: My Life in New Orleans*.

New Orleans

A letter from Larry Amadee, a boy with whom I was raised up with in New Orleans, from the early days when we were both in the Colored Waif's Home for Boys, back of City Park Avenue. Real youngsters. He brought back some real and interesting memories of the good old days and the things that we both knew *all* about. And now his letter. From Chicago, Ill.—May 6th, 1968. As follows—

To the King of Trumpeters and the entire musical world. None other than Louis (Dipper) Gatemouth Armstrong. He's my boyhood pal, and definitely my lifelong friend and idol. Papa, I am feeling fairly good physically. Hoping you and your family are enjoying everything that life can offer.

I am indeed very sorry that I cannot make the trip to our good old home town (New Orleans). (Smile.)

Louis, I was down there for the Mardi gras a little over two weeks. I had a wonderful time during my stay. The celebration of 250 years Birth of Jazz was without a doubt the greatest of all events in the history of New Orleans. Out of all the trips that I have made in the past 50 years—the celebration of 250 years of Birth of Jazz was the greatest.

I have followed you all through your musical career—more than anybody else. You and I met in Professor Jones' Waif's Home for Bad Boys, the year of 1913. Remember?—Real youngsters. Back in those days, Buckeye Joe—King Oliver—was my favorite on cornet. We all named him Buckeye because he had a cataract on his eye and it seemed that he used to buck that eye when he would hit those fine high notes. And he could really hit them in those days.

(Bunk) Willie Johnson was No. "2" on my list. I didn't know very much about Buddy Bolden. Later in my teenage days I heard of him. I was told that he could blow the cornet so loud and strong until you could hear his cornet for miles and miles, and he went crazy from blowing so loud. That's the story that the old timers told me. Sorry that I did not hear him for myself and own judgement. But everybody said he was a character and blew a lot of horn. Bunk Johnson was a good cornet player with a beautiful tone. Bunk was a neighbor to my father + mother in the

downtown section of New Orleans. That was when I was a kid. My fa-
ther also knew such cornet players as Kid Rena, who also came up in the
Orphanage Home of the Colored Waif Home for Boys with us, who also
turned out to be a real good cornet player. Hit high notes real good for a
long time before he died. There's some more real good cornet players that
I knew also—there were Red Brickay, Sidney Desvigne. Another good
one. And Manuel Perez, (Satch played in his band) *he was a waltz*
and schottische king from Downtown in the 7th Ward, known as a
(Stomp Down) Creole, meaning a full-blooded Creole. Better than black.
He played cornet in the Onward Brass Band alongside King Oliver,
whenever there were parades + funerals. And what a ragtime team they
made. On Labor Day Parades with many brass bands—Joe Oliver and
Manuel Perez would get all of the second liners, the raggedy guys who
followed parades + funerals, especially when they played the tunes
"Panama" and the "Saints." The second liners would applaud and
make the Onward Brass Band play an encore for them—which
was unusual.

Speaking of more good cornetists in our young days, Andrew Kimball.
He was a very good cornetist. He played with Professor John Robichaux
at the St. Catherine Hall, just across the street from the Charity Hall on
Tulane Avenue. He also played in Robichaux's Orchestra at the Lyric
Theater at Iberville and Burgundy. Robichaux had the kind of Orches-
tra that could read music real well at first sight. Robichaux was a superb
violinist and handled his Orchestra and those shows with the greatest of
ease. And since the Lyric Theater was a strictly white theater for genera-
tions and they finally turned it over to the colored people, quite naturally
they had to hire the best musicians. So that was it. Robichaux was
THEE man. All of his musicians were well trained. But the youngsters
filed in the theater to hear Kimble. He was just beautiful.

Now for more cornet players of destination in our teenage days in New
Orleans, there was Buddy Petit, cornet, a good blues man. Especially for
the honky tonks such as Savocca's, Spano's, Buddy Bottly's, etc., where all
of the second rate pimps, whores, gamblers hung out all night. Buddy
was definitely their choice. Especially when he blew those blues for them.
He was also their choice at the Economy Hall. Whenever they gave a ball

in the days of good old ragtime and jazz music, they hired him to play his cornet. Another good cornet player was Papa Celestin, although he blew his cornet from the side of his lips. He always delivered a real beautiful tone. Mellow and very pleasing to the ear. He was the leader of the Tuxedo Brass Band and they really were airtight.

I, Louis Armstrong, had the thrilling pleasure of playing second cornet with Celestin and his Brass Band. When my idol Joe King Oliver sent for me to join his Creole Jazz Band in 1922 in Chicago-Ill, to play second trumpet to him. I had just finished playing a funeral with Celestin and his Tuxedo Brass Band when I received the wire from Papa Joe (the name I always called him). And it was a hard decision for me to leave Tuxedo. My best break down in N.O. [was] with Celestin and at the same time I was playing on the Steamer Sydney—Excursion Boat with Fate Marable's Band. I loved both jobs and was pretty much satisfied. But I loved Joe King Oliver so much, and out of clear skies I find myself immediately after I had finished playing a funeral that day with Tuxedo going to the Illinois Central [Railroad] Station, that is inquiring about my ticket to Chicago. I made up my mind just that quick. Nothing could change it. Joe my idol had sent for me— wow. Fate Marable, Celestin, and the whole Tuxedo Brass Band came to the station with me that day. They said stay home, you are all set here, Joe Oliver's Band is scabbin' in Chicago. I told them these words: Joe Oliver is my idol. I have loved him all my life. He sent for me and whatever he's doing I want to do it with him. Just then I boarded the train with the fish sandwich (trout loaf) that Mayann, my dear mother, had fixed for me and I was on my way to be with the man I musically loved—King Oliver. I did not rest until I saw his smiling face. Although he missed me at the 12th Street Station because my train was late, and he had to go to work with the Creole Jazz Band at the Lincoln Gardens. The railroad where I arrived was at 12th Street + Michigan and the Lincoln Gardens was at 31st Street + Cottage Grove Ave., Chicago. Joe Oliver couldn't wait for the next train that I was to arrive on, so he tipped the porter to be on the lookout for me. The porter put me in a taxicab that would take me to the Gardens. When I got to the Gardens, King Oliver, Johnny Dodds, Honore Dutrey, Lil Hardin, Baby Dodds, Bill Johnson were swinging some tune and it sounded so great until I was almost in doubt whether I should go in the place and report to Papa Joe or just go on back to N.O. on the next train. In fact, from the music that I was hearing I did not think I was good enough to ever sit in the band. Somebody must have told Joe Oliver about my dumbness—standing out there and refusing to come in—so Papa Joe came outside and when he saw me, the first words that he said to me, "Come on IN HEAH, you little dumb sombitch, we've been waiting for your black ass all night. Ha ha." Then I was happy and at home just to hear his voice, and enjoyed every moment with him. Mrs. Stella Oliver, Joe Oliver's wife, was really swell to me. I ate all of my meals with Papa Joe. He liked the kinds of food that I loved and was raised on. We both were raised on soul food. Later about that.—

Now back to Larry Amadee and my choice or our choice of all the pioneers of Ragtime and Jazz Music through the years. In his letter to me, we agreed on everything that he said because it is right. So dig this. We also admired these cornet players. Lee Collins, Red Allen, Guy Kelly, Chris Kelly, Sam Morgan, Punch Miller. They *all* were good cornet players. Some more cornets— Freddie Keppard, Wooden Joe Nicholas (he was Albert Nicholas the great clarinet player's uncle). Maurice Durand was a very good cornetist, but was very much underrated. Larry Amadee sez, *I may be a layman but I am a damn good one.* How true. He took up boxing and training and he did wonders for Joe Louis with Blackburn, that is if you followed Joe Louis's career. Larry also told me *Louis, I am full of good music. I am an uncultivated critic. I know it when I hear it. I can't play it, I always could dance to it very good* (meaning good Jazz.) *Louis Armstrong is a Hall of Fame. Armstrong is a legend. King Oliver won my admiration during my boyhood days. His style hypnotized me. Funeral parades and furniture wagons.* Advertisements. *Our idol the late Joe King Oliver was in Savannah, Georgia.* Stranded after many years illness, an old man. *Louis Armstrong saw him there just before he died* (when Louis [was] touring with Luis Russell's band) *and gave him a lot of money that he had collected on his one night stands, which was a great thrill to Louis Armstrong.* (He said.) *They buried King Oliver in New York and Louis Armstrong was right there at his funeral. He loved that man. He also wept.*

Amadee speaking—*Oliver had extra lungs close to perfection.* When he was young. *My first musical idol. Louis is the second idol. Joe and Louis are really incomparable, musically speaking. Among the old clarinet players the late Johnny Dodds, Joe Oliver's star clarinetist and one of the greatest of all times. The late Big Eye Louis Nelson was one of the greatest.* (In the early years.) *He refused to travel. Barney Bigard, a youngster from N.O., traveled with "Louie" for many years.* Louis Armstrong "sez" he thinks that Barney is the greatest clarinet player that he ever blowed with. Yes, he thinks Barney cut 'em all. Louis did not play any too much with Jimmie Noone, but admits that he is a real good man on the clarinet. He still thinks that Barney is the apple of his eye, clarinetwise. Tio-Picou-Sam Dutrey. Albert Nicholas is also a good clarinetist, said Louis—but I'll still take ol' Barnyard (our pet name for Barney).

Amadee mentions drummers and he's right. We see them eye to eye. Meelie Barnes, Albert Francis (whom I enjoyed working with at Tom Anderson's Restaurant in Paul Dominguez's Band, on Rampart near Canal Street. Early days.)

Some more good drummers whom I am very familiar with—Joe Watson, Pete Lacosso. Red Happy, in our minds the greatest drummer in the jazzland style. He was born great. He could sing, dance, be funny + play those drums better than anybody else. It was really a thrill to watch him work. He always had Something new up his sleeves that was real interesting, yea Red Happy Bolton. He and Black Benny were our choice, especially Louis Armstrong's, of all the all-time drummers in our teenage days in New Orleans. And God knows they were all great drummers. But Redhead Happy and Black Benny were the top characters. But good + great. Now there were other great drummers such—as Zutty Singleton, Paul (Tee Boy) Barbarin. Came up with us. Also played with Luis Russell. *Baby Dodds*—(On the boat with Fate Marable.) Snags, Joe Oliver's old ace. He was exceptionally good and kept Joe Oliver in stitches with laughter every night. He was snaggled toothed and no teeth in the front of his mouth at all. And when he takes a drum solo he looks straight at Joe Oliver and when he smiles at Joe with no teeth, Joe Oliver would crack up so bad, until we almost have to drag him off the bandstand. And we weren't much help, because we're all so tickled with laughing at Snags— we were all too weak to do anything. And it happened every time. Little Mack was a good drummer. Oh boy, he was known for his rhythm. The way he slapped those sticks on those drums was really something else. Joe Lindsey was a young fine drummer. He and I had a teenage band when we were very young. Joe Lindsey, being a nice looking youngster, got wrapped up with one of those big time sporting gals, giving him lots of money. And—well, you can figure out the rest of his life. He died with everything that you could think of. (All kinds of complications.) Chinees (his nickname) was another drummer from the old Economy Hall days. I enjoyed working with him also, but didn't see much of him. I was so busy being around Happy, Black Benny and Snags, did not see or play with the other fellers very much. Of course when I went to Chicago, I ran into another great drummer from New Orleans whom I thought was a real great drummer in Carroll Dickerson's Orchestra (which I played with for Joe Glaser at the Sunset), and that's none other than Tubby Fred Hall. (Minor Hall's brother. Both drummers of old in New Orleans. More about Tubby.) Now there was a drummer in my books who stood up with the best of them, and until this day of modern times. Of course, I must agree with Larry Amadee concerning Black Benny. Outside of being a great drummer and a good musician and our idol, he was a neat and handsome man with a well constructed body. Fearless. Would fight at the drop of the hat and *could* fight. (Story of the Fire Department—the Church + and the guy called Jesus.)

Here's the name of the Dance Hall sections during our young days—as follows—The Economy Hall (downtown across Canal

Street), Co-Operators Hall (ditto), the Winter Garden (up from Canal Street), the Roof Garden (Rampart Street), the Sans Souci Hall (uptown), The Butcher Hill Hall (near the Protection Levee up in Charlton), Bradens Astoria Hotel dance hall (Rampart and Gravier), the Pythian Temple Roof Garden (located on Gravier and Saratoga Streets opposite the old Parish Prison), Pete Lala's Cabaret in Storyville (where Joe Oliver played for many years), Mrs. Cole's Willow Lawn (uptown), where Kid Ory's Band played for a long time. Later Joe Oliver joined them there. Ory + Oliver (or vice versa). The Fairgrounds Battlefield Hall, they also held horse races there. The Artesan Hall (all Creoles) in the 7th Ward, the Perseverance Hall (ditto), the Francs Amis Hall (Creole Section), the Independence Hall (ditto, Elmira Street near St. Claude St.), St. Mary's Hall (the same), Two Honky Tonks (3rd Ward), Savocca's (Poydras and Saratoga), and Spano's (Poydras and Franklin Sts.), Pratts on Dryades + Perdido (later Howard Ave and Dryades St.), Henry Matranga's Honky Tonk (Franklin + Perdido Sts., 3rd Ward), where Armstrong came up, played at Matranga's.

Willie Jackson, singer + comedian, played the Lyric Theater, Iroquois Theater, and Tom Anderson before he came up north. Tom Anderson [was] No. "2", corner of Iberville and Basin St. in Storyville—Red Light District. Lulu White was the Queen of Storyville Red Light District. Louis Clark Wade and Morris Moore were the two big pimps bosses among the colored broads—and Paul Gross was a second rater in line. Butsey Fernandez was the big white pimp. Ludlum, Aaron Harris, Geo. Boe Hog, and Bob Keno were the leading colored gamblers that were well known. The boundary lines of Storyville—Basin Street to North Claiborne, Canal Street to St. Louis Street. Boxing Arenas—the Orleans Athletic Club, Tulane A.C., the Louisiana Auditorium, Pilsbury Garden A.C., Hypodrome A.C., Northside Club, National Baseball, Heineman Park, Tommy Burns Club. Two colored unknown clubs.

A large number of nicknamed characters that made history in the City of New Orleans, La. They fought each other because of hate, jealousy + rivalry. They would gang around different dance halls; there were real bullies in all the wards. In different neighborhoods—Uptown, Downtown, Front of Town, and Back of Town. Said Larry—*I know because I traveled around the city quite a bit in my boyhood days.*

I delivered groceries, drugs, shoes, I also worked on the ice cream wagons. Plus—I attended dances in different parts of the City of N.O. Louis started playing with the best older musicians during the times that I didn't run across him. So he got good real early. As a boy, I did not have much fear. I will arrive at my conclusion by beginning to name some of the well known characters. A good long story to my good friend and idol, Louis Armstrong. I do hope that this long historical story didn't bore you Gate/Satch.

The Memory of the Bullies and Trouble Makers. Black Benny, Jimmy Maker, Yellow Lugene, Dirty Dog, Red Devil, Cheeky Black, Long Head Willie Logan, Roughhouse Cameel.

Second Line Buddies. Nica Deemus, Rawhead, Black Sol, Black Lute, Hobo Crookit, Big Walter Bell, Cocaine Buddy, Ikey Smooth, Jakey Brown, Lips the Camel, Big Sore Dick, Foots Arrel, Nasty Slim.

The Females. Big Vi Green, Mary Meat Market, Funky Stella, Foote Mama, Crosseyed Louise, Mary Jack the Bear, Alberta, Steal Arm Johnny.

Notorious Group. Zeno Green—*he wore those stack ties, nicknamed Stacktie Kid. He owned a little colored hotel at Rampart and Lafayette Sts. and worked at the Iroquois Theater as ticket taker, at Rampart and Perdido Streets. It was a small moving picture house we used to love to go and see Wm. S. Hart and Eddie Polo, etc. 10 cents admission. Raffle nights were on Tuesdays. If you had a lucky number on your ticket, you win a pound of delicious chocolates. Hmmm, but they were good. Redhead Happy played drums there. Kid Green was an ex-prize fighter, [and] won enough money to become owner of the Baton Rouge Hotel—Rampart and Lafayette Streets. Kid Green was also a dog trainer. Green had all of his white teeth pulled out and replaced with all gold teeth. Green bought a Boston bulldog and [had] all of his white teeth pulled and also replaced with gold teeth. Green taught his dog to smile only at white people on Canal Street, and growl and bark at colored people. That was because the white people would tip more money. Green had a gold chain and a blood red jacket on his dog. What a character. P.S. I knew Maurice Durand's mother, father and brothers. They all lived on Lizard Street, downtown in the 9th Ward.*

Special attention Satchmo. Whenever you are on TV programs and wherever you may be in this country, if opportune time presents itself, please dedicate a number to me. My favorite song, "When the Saints Go Marchin' In." Give my regards to all. Sincerely yours in sports—
Larry Amadee
[address and phone number in Chicago]
We both were born on national holidays. Two of New Orleans' famous sons. Louis Armstrong, July 4, 1900, and Larry Amadee, Christmas December 25, 1898. Both men have the same initials— L.A. and L.A.
's all/more—
Fate Marable's Band on the Mississippi Excursion Steamboats. Our opening number was "In the Land of Beginning Again."

Discography

We include the discography prepared for the original edition of this book, which consists largely of LPs, as well as a more contemporary list of CDs. Records of every kind go in and out of print with alarming rapidity, but often have an afterlife in specialty stores. Serious—or obsessive—Louis Armstrong lovers may find several LPs well worth searching for, notably the Smithsonian anthologies; Decca's *Rare Items, Satchmo at Symphony Hall,* and *Satchmo: A Musical Autobiography*; and anything in the original Columbia CL series, if only for the warm acoustical sound. Much of this music may be found on European imports if not in domestic anthologies. The CD has filled in many blanks while neglecting many others; overall, the major American labels have a long way to go to do justice to the Armstrong catalog.

DISCOGRAPHY 1 (1988)

Albums are listed in rough chronological order within each section. Catalogue numbers denote LPs, though some compact discs are also included. The period of time covered by an album is given at the end of the entry, unless that information is part of the title. I've tried to limit repetitions and have focused on domestic albums that were in print during the past decade, though there are of necessity many exceptions. As all jazz lovers know, American record companies have failed to prepare definitive editions of Armstrong's major work. The long-playing record has been with us forty years and may soon be obsolete, but many of Armstrong's most acclaimed performances—most notably those controlled by Columbia and MCA—have never appeared on American LPs. His recordings with blues singers, for example, have been collated in France, England, Australia, Japan, and other nations, but never in the United States. Nor is there a satisfactory U.S. collection of his recordings with Fletcher Henderson. On those albums where Armstrong is heard on half or less than half the selections, I've specified the number.

The Apprentice Years/
Sideman Recordings 1923–1930

Louis Armstrong and King Oliver (Milestone M-47017). With King Oliver's Creole Jazz Band, Red Onion Jazz Babies. 1923–24.

King Oliver and His Creole Jazz Band 1923 (Smithsonian R001).

Louis Armstrong and Sidney Bechet in New York 1923–1925 (Smithsonian R026). With Clarence Williams's Blue Five, Red Onion Jazz Babies, Fletcher Henderson, Maggie Jones, Trixie Smith, Grant and Wilson, Perry Bradford's Jazz Phools.

Young Louis the Sideman (1924–1927) (MCA 1301). With Fletcher Henderson, Perry Bradford's Jazz Phools, Erskine Tate's Vendome Orchestra, Lil's Hot Shots, Jimmy Bertrand's Washboard Wizards, Johnny Dodds's Black Bottom Stompers.

Johnny Dodds, *The Spirit of New Orleans 1926–1927* (MCA 1328). Two selections.

Fletcher Henderson, *A Study in Frustration* (France, CBS 66423). Nine selections. 1924–25.

Fletcher Henderson, *Developing an American Orchestra 1923–1937* (Smithsonian R006). Five selections. 1924–25.

Fletcher Henderson, *The Pathé Sessions* (Australia, Swaggie 803). Seven selections. 1924–25.

Fletcher Henderson, *First Impressions* (MCA 1310). Two selections. 1924.

Louis Armstrong and Fletcher Henderson's Orchestra (England, VJM VLP-60). 1924–25.

Ma Rainey (Milestone M-47021). Three selections. 1924.

Bessie Smith, *The Empress* (Columbia G-30818). Six selections. 1925.

Bessie Smith, *Nobody's Blues But Mine* (Columbia G-31093). Three selections. 1925.

Rare Recordings of the Twenties, Vol. 1 (France, CBS 64218). With Maggie Jones, Nolan Walsh, Clara Smith, Sippie Wallace. 1924–27.

Rare Recordings of the Twenties, Vol. 2 (France, CBS 65379). With Clarence Williams's Blue Five, Hociel Thomas. 1924–25.

Rare Recordings of the Twenties, Vol. 3 (France, CBS 65380). With Lillie Delk Christian, Bertha "Chippie" Hill. 1926–28.

Rare Recordings of the Twenties, Vol. 4 (France, CBS 65421). With Blanche Calloway, Baby Mack, Hociel Thomas, Bertha "Chippie" Hill, Sippie Wallace, Victoria Spivey. 1925–29.

Jimmie Rodgers on Record: America's Blue Yodeler (Smithsonian R034). One selection. 1930.

Louis Armstrong Special (France, CBS 65251). With Carroll Dickerson, Seger Ellis, Louis Armstrong and His Orchestra. 1928–32.

The Armstrong Era 1925–1932

Armstrong's OKeh recordings are the foundation of the jazz art. Incredibly, no complete edition exists. The *V.S.O.P.* series is the most comprehensive: It has all 128 titles by the Hot 5, Hot 7, Savoy Ballroom Five, and the orchestras (Les Hite's and Zilner Randolph's) Armstrong fronted, but no alternate takes. An Amer-

164

Discography

ican edition announced by Columbia is apparently going to duplicate the *V.S.O.P.* programming, but the digital remastering on
the first volume is disappointingly shrill. The remastering on the
BBC "Jazz Classics in Digital Stereo" anthology is superb, and
one can hope that engineer Robert Parker will eventually do all
the OKehs; the necessity of relying on Europe for this level of
craftsmanship is a disgrace that protectionism won't cure. The
remaining Columbia and DRG albums are solid anthologies of
OKeh selections (with alternate takes) and have been in print for
many years, though the new Columbia series may knock them out.
The Smithsonian collection duplicates Columbia's Armstrong-
Hines volume and has many other selections as well. Except for
two alternate takes, the Armstrong performances on the two
DRG albums are combined on a single compact disc (DRG
CDXP 8450).

~

V.S.O.P. Vol. 1/2 (France, CBS 88001). 1925–27.
V.S.O.P. Vol. 3/4 (France, CBS 88002). 1927–28.
V.S.O.P. Vol. 5/6 (France, CBS 88003). 1928–30.
V.S.O.P. Vol. 7/8 (France, CBS 88004). 1930–32.
The Hot 5s, Volume 1 (Columbia CJ 44049). 1925–26.
Great Original Performances 1923–1931 (England, BBC REB 597).
Louis Armstrong and His Hot 5 (Columbia CL 851). 1925–27.
Louis Armstrong and His Hot 7 (Columbia CL 852). 1927.
Louis Armstrong and Earl Hines (Columbia CL 853). 1928.
Louis Armstrong Favorites (Columbia CL 854). 1929–31.
Louis Armstrong and Earl Hines 1928 (Smithsonian R002). With
    Lillie Delk Christian, Carroll Dickerson.
Louis & the Big Bands 1928–30 (DRG Swing 8450).
Louis Armstrong, Jack Purvis, *Satchmo Style 1929–30* (DRG
    Swing 8451). Eight selections.

The Big Band Years 1932–1945

The Decca recordings represent a radical change from the OKehs, but the best of them are every bit as radiant, and they contain much of Armstrong's finest singing and most exhilarating trumpet, as well as many treasurable novelties—including visits with other Decca artists. Unfortunately, MCA, which owns Decca, has been rather nonchalant about making them available here. A comprehensive edition was issued in Australia by Swaggie, called *The Louis Armstrong Orchestra 1935–41: A Chronological Study*, and most of the material was released on a series of albums in France, some of which were briefly distributed in U.S. versions. For most American jazz enthusiasts, the Deccas remain a treasure not yet fully savored. I've included *Rare Items*—although it's been out of print for many years (most of the selections are on MCA 1312) and was electrically sabotaged for stereo—because its release was a revelation in the 1960s and for its influential liner notes by Dan Morgenstern. The six performances recorded in Paris in 1934, on Musicmouth, are also on Onyx, which has an alternate take of "St. Louis Blues," but not the other sessions from the European tour. The Bluebird reissue is exemplary.

~

Young Louis Armstrong 1932–1933 (Bluebird AXM2-5519).
European Tour 1933–1934 (France, Musicmouth 1900).
Tootin' through the Roof: Volume 2 (Onyx 213). Seven selections. 1934.
Back in New York (1935) (MCA 1304).
Rare Items (1935–1944) (Decca DL 79225).
Swing That Music 1936–1938 (MCA 1312).
Satchmo's Collector's Items 1936–1937 (MCA 1322).
Satchmo's Discoveries 1936–1938 (MCA 1326).

More Satchmo's Way (1938) (France, MCA 510.104).
Jeepers Creepers 1938–1939 (France, MCA 510.108).
Harlem Stomp 1939–1941 (France, MCA 510.113).
Heah Me Talkin' to Ya 1939–1941 (France, MCA 510.064).
Satchmo For Ever! 1935–1945 (MCA 1334).

High Society: Louis and Friends 1932–1961

Louis in the 1930s (Collector's Classics 26). Jam session with Jack Teagarden, Bud Freeman, Fats Waller. Radio and film tracks. 1932–42.

New Discoveries (Pumpkin 109). With the Mills Brothers, Frank Sinatra, Benny Goodman, Duke Ellington, All Stars, others. Radio and TV broadcasts. 1937–61.

Louis with Guest Stars (MCA 1306). With Sidney Bechet, Billie Holiday, the Mills Brothers, Ella Fitzgerald. 1938–49.

Midnight at V-Disc (Pumpkin 103). With Jack Teagarden, Bobby Hackett, Lou McGarity, others. Four selections. 1944.

The First Esquire All-American Jazz Concert (Radiola 2MR-5051). With Roy Eldridge, Jack Teagarden, Coleman Hawkins, Art Tatum, others. Concert broadcast. 1944.

The Second Esquire All-American Jazz Concert (England, Saga E-6925). With Benny Goodman and Duke Ellington. Radio broadcast. One selection. 1945.

Havin' Fun (Sounds Rare SR 5009). With Bing Crosby, Joe Venuti, Jack Teagarden. Radio broadcasts. 1949–50.

More Fun (Sounds Rare SR 5010). With Bing Crosby, All Stars, studio orchestra. Radio broadcasts. 1951.

Ella and Louis (Compact disc: Verve 825 373-2). With Ella Fitzgerald and the Oscar Peterson Quartet. 1956.

Ella and Louis Again (Compact disc: Verve 825-374-2). With Ella Fitzgerald and the Oscar Peterson Quartet. 1957.

Porgy and Bess (Verve VE-2-2057). With Ella Fitzgerald and the Russ Garcia Orchestra. 1957.

Louis Armstrong Meets Oscar Peterson (Compact disc: Verve 825 713-2). With the Oscar Peterson Quartet. 1957.

And the Dukes of Dixieland (Audiofidelity AFDS-5924). 1958–60.

Great Alternatives (Chiaroscuro 2003). With the Dukes of Dixieland. 1958–60.

Sweetheart (Chiaroscuro 2006). With the Dukes of Dixieland. 1959.

Bing and Satchmo (MGM E-3882). With Bing Crosby. 1960.

The Real Ambassadors (Columbia OS 2250). With the All Stars, Carmen McRae, Lambert, Hendricks & Ross, Dave Brubeck. 1961.

Together for the First Time/The Great Reunion (Mobile Fidelity 2-807). With Duke Ellington. 1961.

The All Stars Plus 1946–1971

Armstrong's future was sewn up at the 1947 Town Hall concert, when he introduced to great acclaim the small combo that would set the pattern for the various editions of his All Stars. RCA has never issued the entire concert in the U.S., though it was recently issued in France. A compact disc version of *Pops*, subtitled "The 1940s Small-Band Sides" (6378-2-RB), has fifteen of the album's thirty-two selections, plus five numbers from Town Hall (including one, Teagarden's brilliant "St. James Infirmary," on which Armstrong doesn't play), which suggests how inept the custodians of America's classic music can be. Far more egregious are the new Columbia versions of the W. C. Handy and Fats Waller albums; each a montage of original cuts and alternate takes, they masquerade as the much superior original editions—which have now become collector's items. I've noted whether an album presents Armstrong with his All Stars or in another musical setting. Albums identified here and in the preceding category as radio, concert, and TV broadcasts are mostly of doubtful legality but high musical quality.

∽

Pops (Bluebird 5920-1-RB). Big band, All Stars. 1946–47.

With Edmond Hall's All-Stars (Alamac QSR 2411). The Edmond Hall Sextet. Concert broadcast. 1947.

The Complete Town Hall Concert, 1947 (France, RCA NL89746-2). All Stars.

Satchmo at Symphony Hall (MCA2 4057). All Stars. 1947.

Basin Street Blues (France, Jazz Club 2MO56-78139). All Stars, guests. Radio and TV broadcasts. 1947–58.

Reminiscin' with Louis (Italy, Queen Disc 004). Concert, radio broadcasts. All Stars. 1947–50.

At the Eddie Condon Floorshow 1949 (Italy, Queen Disc 010). Concert broadcasts. All Stars and guests.

The All Stars in Philadelphia 1948–1949 (Jazz Archives JA-20). Concert. All Stars.

Satchmo's Golden Favorites (Decca DL 74137). All Stars, choir. 1949–58.

Satchmo Serenades (Decca DL 8211). Sy Oliver Orchestra. 1949–53.

Satchmo Serenades (MCA 1316). Sy Oliver, Toots Camarata, Gordon Jenkins Orchestras. 1949–54.

Old Favorites 1950–1957 (MCA 1335). All Stars.

In Concert at the Pasadena Civic Auditorium (GNP Crescendo 9050). All Stars. 1951.

Plays W. C. Handy (Original: Columbia CSP JCL 591). All Stars. 1954.

Plays W. C. Handy (Columbia CJ 40242). All Stars. 1954.

Rare Performances of the 50's and the 60's (France, CBS 88669). All Stars, Lotte Lenya, Dave Brubeck, Newport International Jazz Band. 1954–66.

At the Crescendo (MCA2 4013). All Stars. 1955.

Satch Plays Fats (Original: Columbia CSP JCL 708). All Stars. 1955.

Satch Plays Fats (Columbia CJ 40378). All Stars. 1955.

Ambassador Satch (Columbia CSP JCL 840). All Stars. 1955.

Chicago Concert (Columbia C2-36426). All Stars. 1956.

Satchmo the Great (Columbia CSP JCL 1077). All Stars, New York Philharmonic directed by Leonard Bernstein. 1956.

Satchmo: A Musical Autobiography Volume 1 (MCA2 4173). All Stars, guests, big band. 1956–57.

Satchmo: A Musical Autobiography Volume 2 (MCA 4174). All Stars, guests, big band. 1956–57.

Louis and the Angels (Decca DL 8488). Sy Oliver Orchestra and choir. 1957.

Verve Silver Collection (Compact disc: Verve 823 446-2). Russ Garcia Orchestra. 1957.

Louis and the Good Book (MCA 1300). All Stars plus organ and choir. 1958.

Satchmo Plays King Oliver (Audiofidelity AFLP 1930). All Stars. 1959.

Snake Rag (Chiaroscuro CR 2002). All Stars. 1959.

Master of Jazz (Storyville SLP-4101). All Stars. 1962.

Hello, Dolly! (MCA 538). All Stars plus banjo. 1963–64.

The Essential Louis Armstrong (Vanguard VSD 91/92). All Stars. 1965.

Louis (Mercury SR 61081). All Stars plus banjo. 1965–66.

What a Wonderful World (MCA 2504). All Stars, big band, and strings. 1967–68.

I Will Wait for You (Brunswick 754136). Studio orchestra and choir. 1968.

Disney Songs the Satchmo Way (Buena Vista 4044). The All Stars plus studio orchestra with strings and choir. 1968.

Greatest Hits Recorded Live (Brunswick 754169). All Stars. 1968.

And His Friends (Flying Dutchman AMS-12009). Big band, strings, choir, Leon Thomas. 1970.

Country and Western (Avco Embassy AVE-33022). The Nashville Rhythm Section. 1970.

"The Night Before Christmas" (Continental 45-CR 1001). A reading of the poem. 1971.

Discography 2 (2001)

This list follows the original format and does not duplicate information when the CD is an exact match for the LP (though the addition of "bonus tracks" is noted). Nor does it include catalog numbers, which are no longer necessary for ordering discs in virtual or actual shops. Most early Armstrong records, including the Clarence Williams sessions with Sidney Bechet, can be found on an apparently endless European series called The Chronological Classics, distributed to the larger record chains.

The Apprentice Years/
Sideman Recordings 1923–1930

Louis Armstrong and King Oliver (Milestone).

King Oliver, *Volume One 1922 to 1929* (Jazz Classics in Digital Stereo). Ten selections, 1923.

Fletcher Henderson, *A Study in Frustration* (Columbia/Legacy).

Fletcher Henderson and Louis Armstrong, 1924–1925 (Timeless).

Johnny Dodds, *South Side Chicago Jazz* (MCA). Six selections, 1927.

Ma Rainey (Milestone).

Bessie Smith, *The Complete Recordings, Vol. 2* (Columbia/Legacy). Nine selections, 1925.

Louis Armstrong and the Blues Singers, 1924–1930. (Affinity). Six discs—the complete works, from Europe, of course.

Louis Armstrong, *Portrait of the Artist as a Young Man, 1923–1934* (Columbia/Legacy). More than a third of the eighty-one selections in this superb collection are sideman performances, notably an assortment of blues singers—including the anomalous track with Jimmie Rodgers.

The Armstrong Era 1925–1932

To pick up from Discography 1, the OKehs have now been issued complete, though with less than entirely satisfactory results. The initial attempt by Columbia, referred to in my original comments, was all but unlistenable and the individual discs, still in shops, ought to be shunned. A second attempt shows a marked improvement and can be recommended to anyone with the slightest interest in American music. *The Complete Hot 5 and Hot 7 Recordings* includes alternate takes, but not the big band tracks with Hite and Randolph (still available in the earlier CD series and listed below). The sound, however, despite some pitch corrections, is highly uneven and many selections are marred by hiss, distortion, and digital iciness in the higher frequencies that do not exist on the old Columbia LPs; perhaps the most jarring track is "Willie the Weeper." The JSP series, engineered with innovative transfers by England's John R. T. Davies, has a warmer, fuller, more realistic sound that approximates the vinyl experience. JSP, which does not include alternate takes, is more expensive and is most easily found online; I much prefer it.

∾

The Complete Hot 5 and 7 Recordings (Columbia/Legacy). Four discs, 1925–29.
Hot 5s and 7s Volume One (JSP). 1925–26.
Hot 5s and 7s Volume Two (JSP). 1927.
Hot 5s and 7s Volume Three (JSP). 1928–29.
Big Bands 1930–31, Volume One (JSP).
Big Bands 1931–32, Volume Two (JSP).
Louis In New York, Vol. 5 (Columbia/Legacy). 1929.
St. Louis Blues, Vol. 6 (Columbia/Legacy). 1929–30.
You're Driving Me Crazy, Vol. 7 (Columbia/Legacy). 1930–31.
Louis & The Big Bands 1928–30 (Disques Swing).

The Big Band Years 1932–1945

RCA Victor, which initially released CDs with boxy sound that lost most of the high and low frequencies (as in the single disc anthologies listed below), has greatly improved over the years and did right by Armstrong with its essential *Complete* edition. Decca still has a long way to go, but the *Highlights* collection is a good place to begin.

~

The Complete RCA Victor Recordings (BMG Classics). Four discs, 1932–56.

Laughin' Louis (Bluebird). 1932–33.

Pops: The 1940s Small-Band Sides (Bluebird). 1946–47.

Highlights from His Decca Years (Decca). Two discs, 1924–57.

Rhythm Saved the World (Decca). 1935–36.

Louis Armstrong & His Orchestra, Vol. 2: Heart Full of Rhythm (Decca). 1936–38.

Louis Armstrong & His Orchestra, Vol. 3: Pocketful of Dreams (Decca). 1938.

On the Sunny Side of the Street: Live in '43 (Jass).

High Society: Louis and Friends 1932–1961

Fun with Bing & Louis (Jasmine). Highlights from Armstrong's appearances on Crosby's radio show, 1949–51.

Bing & Louis Havin' Fun (Jazz Unlimited). Complete Crosby shows, with Ella Fitzgerald, Jack Teagarden, Joe Venuti, Peggy Lee.

Bing & Louis Havin' More Fun (Jazz Unlimited). Complete Crosby shows, with Jack Teagarden, Joe Venuti, Dinah Shore.

Louis Armstrong, Bing Crosby, Rosemary Clooney, *That Travelin' Two-Beat* (Axis). Includes the 1960 LP with Bing Crosby.

Midnights at V-Disc (Jazz Unlimited). With Jack Teagarden, Bobby Hackett.

The Complete Ella Fitzgerald and Louis Armstrong (Verve). Three discs (includes *Porgy and Bess*), 1956–57.

Ella and Louis (Verve).

Ella and Louis Again (Verve).

Louis Armstrong Meets Oscar Peterson (Verve).

Let's Do It: Best of the Verve Years (Verve). With Oscar Peterson, Ella Fitzgerald, two discs, 1956–65.

Lotte Lenya Sings Kurt Weill/American Theater Songs (Sony Classical). One selection, plus rehearsal tape, 1955.

Satchmo and the Dukes of Dixieland (Happy Times). 1959.

Dave Brubeck, *The Real Ambassadors* (Columbia/Legacy).

Louis Armstrong and Duke Ellington, *The Great Summit/The Master Takes* (Roulette Jazz).

Louis Armstrong and Duke Ellington, *The Making of the Great Summit* (Roulette Jazz). Running tape with false starts, etc.

The All Stars Plus 1946–1971

The Complete Decca Studio Louis Armstrong All Stars (Mosaic). Six discs, 1950–58.

Louis Armstrong at MGM: Now You Has Jazz (Rhino). Film scores, 1951–65.

An American Icon (Hip-O). Three discs, 1946–68.

Louis Armstrong Sings: Back Through the Years (MCA). Two discs, 1938–67.

The California Concerts (Decca). Four discs, combines Pasadena and Crescendo albums, 1951–55. Bonus tracks.

The Best of the Decca Years, Vol. One (MCA). 1937–56.

Louis Armstrong of New Orleans (Decca). 1927–50.

The Best of Louis Armstrong: The Millennium Collection (MCA). 1949–68.

Ambassador Satch (Columbia/Legacy).

The Great Chicago Concert (Columbia/Legacy). Two discs, 1956. Bonus tracks.

Satchmo the Great (Columbia/Legacy). Bonus tracks.

Louis Armstrong Plays W. C. Handy (Columbia/Legacy). Bonus tracks.

Satch Plays Fats (Columbia/Legacy). Bonus tracks.

16 Most Requested Songs (Columbia/Legacy). 1955–66.
The Essential Louis Armstrong (Verve). 1957–66.
Mack the Knife (Pablo). 1957.
The Sullivan Years (TVT). 1956–62.
Americans in Sweden, 1959 (Tax).
Happy Birthday Louis! (Omega). 1960.
Master of Jazz/Live in Chicago, 1962 (Mobile Fidelity).
Hello, Dolly! (MCA)
Greatest Hits (RCA Victor). 1933–70.

Bibliography

A comprehensive bibliography of Louis Armstrong, one of the most written about performers of the century, will require a book of its own and be a valuable addition to the jazz library. The following highly selective list of books and articles provides a variety of interpretations, musical and biographical, as well as a massive amount of information. I've used the original editions except when they've been revised or expanded. Most of the major works are in catalogue from Da Capo, Greenwood, Limelight, and other reprint presses. Three spoken-word recordings are also included here, rather than in the discography. For reasons of space, I've omitted all liner notes, newspaper stories, concert programs, and publicity handouts (a useful source in Armstrong's case), and—with a few exceptions—articles in jazz magazines.

Allen, Walter C. *Hendersonia*. New Jersey: Jazz Monographs No. 4, 1973.

Armstrong, Lil Hardin. *Satchmo and Me* (recording). New York: Riverside 12–120.

Armstrong, Louis. *Swing That Music*. London: Longmans, 1936.

Armstrong, Louis. *Satchmo: My Life in New Orleans*. New York: Prentice-Hall, 1954.

Armstrong, Louis. "Storyville—Where the Blues Were Born," *True*, November 1947.

Armstrong, Louis. "Europe—With Kicks," *Holiday*, June 1950.

Armstrong, Louis. "Jazz on a High Note," *Esquire*, December 1951.

Armstrong, Louis. "Why I Like Dark Women," *Ebony*, August 1954.

Armstrong, Louis. "It's Tough to Top a Million," *Our World*, August 1956.

Armstrong, Louis. "Good-bye To All Of You From . . . ," *Esquire*, December 1969.

Armstrong, Louis. "Scanning the History of Jazz," *Esquire*, December 1971.

Armstrong, Louis. *Satchmo* (recording). Glendale: Varese 8106.

Armstrong, Louis. *Talks about Louis Armstrong* (recording). Anaheim: Mark-56 690.

Armstrong, Lucille, with Pat Cunningham. "Life with Louie!" *Color*, December 1952.

Avakian, George. "Louis Armstrong." Shapiro, Nat, and Nat Hentoff. *The Jazz Makers*. New York: Rinehart, 1957.

Bankhead, Tallulah. "The World's Greatest Musician," *Ebony*, December 1952.

Barker, Danny. *A Life in Jazz*. New York: Oxford, 1986.

Basie, Count, and Albert Murray. *Good Morning Blues: The Autobiography of Count Basie*. New York: Random House, 1985.

Bechet, Sidney. *Treat It Gentle*. London: Cassell, 1960.

Bergreen, Laurence. *Louis Armstrong: An Extravagant Life*. New York: Broadway Books, 1997.

Berrett, Joshua, editor. *The Louis Armstrong Companion*. New York: Schirmer Books, 1999.

Bigard, Barney, with Barry Martyn. *With Louis and the Duke*. New York: Oxford, 1986.

Black, Charles L., Jr. *The Humane Imagination*. Woodbridge: Ox Bow Press, 1986.

Blesh, Rudi. *Shining Trumpets*. New York: Knopf, 1946.

Borneman, Ernest. "'Bop Will Kill Business Unless It Kills Itself First'—Louis Armstrong," *Down Beat*, April 7, 1948.

Brooks, Edward. *The Bessie Smith Companion*. New York: Da Capo, 1982.

Brothers, Thomas, editor. *Louis Armstrong in His Own Words*. New York: Oxford, 1999.

Caffey, H. David. "The Musical Style of Louis Armstrong," *Journal of Jazz Studies*, Fall 1975.

Callender, Red, with Elaine Cohen. *Unfinished Dream: The Musical World of Red Callender*. London: Quartet, 1985.

Chilton, John. *Sidney Bechet: The Wizard of Jazz*. New York: Oxford, 1987.

Clayton, Buck, with Nancy Miller Elliott. *Buck Clayton's Jazz World*. New York: Oxford, 1987.

Collier, James Lincoln. *Louis Armstrong: An American Genius*. New York: Oxford, 1983.

Condon, Eddie, with Thomas Sugrue. *We Called It Music*. rev. ed. New York: Da Capo, 1988.

Crouch, Stanley. "Laughin' Louis," *The Village Voice*, August 14, 1978.

Crowther, Bruce, and Mike Pinfold. *The Jazz Singers*. Poole: Blandford Press, 1986.

Dance, Stanley. *The World of Swing*. New York: Scribners, 1974.

Dance, Stanley. *The World of Earl Hines*. New York: Scribners, 1977.

Ellington, Duke. *Music Is My Mistress*. Garden City, N.Y.: Doubleday, 1973.

Feather, Leonard. *From Satchmo to Miles*. New York: Stein and Day, 1972.

Feather, Leonard. *The Jazz Years: Earwitness to an Era*. London: Quartet, 1986.

Feather, Leonard. "Pops Pops Top on Sloppy Bop," *Metronome*, October 1949.

Ferguson, Otis. *The Otis Ferguson Reader*. Highland Park: December Press, 1982.

Finkelstein, Sidney. *Jazz: A People's Music*. New York: Citadel, 1948.

Freeman, Bud. *You Don't Look Like a Musician*. Detroit: Belamp, 1974.

Giddins, Gary. *Bing Crosby: A Pocketful of Dreams—The Early Years, 1903–1940*. Boston: Little, Brown, 2001.

Giddins, Gary. *Visions of Jazz: The First Century*. New York: Oxford, 1998.

Giddins, Gary, Dan Morgenstern, and Stanley Crouch. "Armstrong at 85," *The Village Voice*, August 27, 1985.

Gillespie, Dizzy, with Al Fraser. *To Be or Not to Bop*. Garden City, N.Y.: Doubleday, 1979.

Gioia, Ted. *The Imperfect Art*. New York: Oxford, 1988.

Gitler, Ira. *Swing to Bop*. New York: Oxford, 1985.

Glenn, Tyree. "Unforgettable Satchmo," *Reader's Digest*, December 1971.

Goddard, Chris. *Jazz Away from Home*. London: Paddington Press, 1979.

Goffin, Robert. *Horn of Plenty: The Story of Louis Armstrong*. New York: Allen, Towne & Heath, 1947.

Hadlock, Richard. *Jazz Masters of the 20's*. New York: Macmillan, 1965.

Hammond, John, with Irving Townsend. *John Hammond on Record*. New York: Summit, 1977.

Harrison, Max, Charles Fox, and Eric Thacker. *The Essential Jazz Records*. Westport: Greenwood Press, 1984.

Hentoff, Nat. *Jazz Is*. New York: Random House, 1975.

Hentoff, Nat, and Albert J. McCarthy. *Jazz*. New York: Rinehart, 1959.

Hodes, Art, and Chadwick Hansen. *Selections from the Gutter*. Berkeley: University of California, 1977.

Hodier, Andre. *Jazz: Its Evolution and Essence*. New York: Grove Press, 1956.

Jones, LeRoi. *Blues People*. New York: Morrow, 1963.

Jones, Max. *Talking Jazz*. New York: W. W. Norton, 1988.

Jones, Max, and John Chilton. *Louis: The Louis Armstrong Story 1900–1971.* rev. ed. New York: Da Capo, 1988.

Kaminsky, Max, with V. E. Hughes. *My Life in Jazz.* New York: Harper and Row, 1963.

King, Larry. "Everybody's Louis Armstrong," *Harper's,* November 1967.

Kolodin, Irving. "All God's Chillun Got Fun," *Americana,* February 1933.

Lyttelton, Humphrey. *The Best of Jazz.* New York: Taplinger, 1979.

Lyttelton, Humphrey. *The Best of Jazz II.* New York: Taplinger, 1982.

Marquis, Donald M. *In Search of Buddy Bolden.* Baton Rouge: Louisiana State University Press, 1978.

Matthews, Jim. *Satchmo.* Hollywood: Collector's Copy, 1971.

McCarthy, Albert. *Louis Armstrong.* London: Cassell, 1959.

Merryman, Richard. *Louis Armstrong—a Self-Portrait.* New York: Eakins Press, 1971.

Mezzrow, Mezz, and Bernard Wolfe. *Really the Blues.* New York: Random House, 1946.

Miller, Mark H., editor. *Louis Armstrong: A Cultural Legacy.* New York: The Queens Museum of Art, 1994.

Millstein, Gilbert. "Africa Harks to Satch's Horn," *The New York Times Magazine,* November 20, 1960.

Morgenstern, Dan. "Book Review. Louis Armstrong: An American Genius," *Annual Review of Jazz Studies 3,* 1985.

Morgenstern, Dan, and Ole Brask. *Jazz People.* New York: Abrams, 1976.

Murray, Albert. *Stomping the Blues.* New York: McGraw-Hill, 1976.

Ostransky, Leon. *Jazz City.* Englewood Cliffs, N.J.: Prentice-Hall, 1978.

Panassie, Hughes. *Louis Armstrong.* New York: Scribners, 1971.

Pinfold, Mike. *Louis Armstrong.* New York: Universe Books, 1987.

Rose, Al. *Storyville, New Orleans.* University, Alabama: University of Alabama Press, 1974.

Rose, Al, and Edmond Souchon. *New Orleans Jazz: A Family Album.* rev. ed. Baton Rouge: Louisiana State University Press, 1984.

Russell, William. "Louis Armstrong." Ramsey, Frederick, Jr., and Charles Edward Smith. *Jazzmen.* New York: Harcourt, Brace, 1939.

Sales, Grover. *Jazz: America's Classical Music.* Englewood Cliffs, N.J.: Prentice-Hall, 1984.

Schuller, Gunther. *Early Jazz: Its Roots and Musical Development.* New York: Oxford, 1968.

Shapiro, Nat, and Nat Hentoff. *Hear Me Talkin' to Ya.* New York: Rinehart, 1955.

Smith, Charles Edward, with Frederick Ramsey, Jr., Charles Payne Rogers, and William Russell. *The Jazz Record Book.* New York: Smith & Durrell, 1942.

Smith, Jay D., and Len Guttridge. *Jack Teagarden: The Story of a Jazz Maverick.* London: Cassell, 1960.

Stearns, Marshall. *The Story of Jazz.* rev. ed. New York: Oxford, 1970.

Stewart, Rex. *Jazz Masters of the 30's.* New York: Macmillan, 1972.

Stratemann, Dr. Klaus. *Louis Armstrong on the Screen.* Copenhagen: Jazz Media, 1996.

Teagarden, Jack. "The World's Greatest Horn Player," *Varsity,* December 1948.

Ward, Geoffrey C. *Jazz.* New York: Knopf, 2000.

Westerberg, Hans. *Boy From New Orleans: A Discography of Louis "Satchmo" Armstrong.* Copenhagen: Jazzmedia, 1981.

Williams, Martin. *Jazz Masters of New Orleans.* New York: Macmillan, 1967.

Williams, Martin. *The Jazz Tradition.* rev. ed. New York: Oxford, 1983.

Wright, Laurie, Walter C. Allen, and Brian A. L. Rust. *King Oliver.* Essex: Storyville, 1987.

Acknowledgments

Many hands contributed to this book, chiefly those of Phoebe Jacobs, the publicist and a close friend of Lucille Armstrong's. In 1974, Phoebe arranged for me to interview Mrs. Armstrong, who died in 1983. A couple of years later, she invited me to visit the Armstrong house in Corona, Queens, and to examine photo albums, tapes, and papers. At the time, I was working with a packager, Toby Byron, and we prepared to produce a photo book, which was superbly designed by Kathleen and Linda Gates, and a documentary film, which subsequently debuted on PBS. My biggest debt to Phoebe is for her foresight in preserving copies of the manuscripts identified here as *Archive*, entrusted to her as part of the Lucille Armstrong Collection; they had never been accessed before and would have been otherwise unavailable to me, as the Armstrong house was taken over by Queens College in 1987, and my access curtailed.

I have long hoped that the text might escape the elaborate design of the original volume and be allowed to stand on its own, not incidentally providing me with the opportunity to make some corrections and revisions. I am grateful to Andrea Schulz and Da Capo Press for allowing me to do just that.

My thanks to Dave Gold and Oscar Cohen, executives along with Phoebe Jacobs of the Louis Armstrong estate. In searching out documents, we employed the services of attorney William T. Abbott, Jr., who helped me acquire Armstrong's FBI files as well as information regarding the Milne Municipal Boys' Home. Harold S. Kaye provided me with Armstrong's passport application and Mama Lucy's marriage license. Writer Tad Jones, who is now working on a full-scale Armstrong biography, sussed out census reports and followed leads (chiefly Louis's, in a letter to Robert Goffin) that brought him to the baptismal registry of the Sacred Heart of Jesus Church and certification of the great man's true birthdate.

Al Rose and his wife, Diana Rose, who know the jazz-related significance of every house and street in New Orleans, provided guided tours of the city. Eddie Edwards, of the Louis Armstrong Foundation, guided us to and through Boutte. The near-legendary archivist and writer Bill Russell was most generous with his comprehensive files, which include articles not found in institutional archives. Danny Barker and his wife, Blue Lu Barker, were most hospitable. Al, Bill, and the Barkers have all passed away, as have others on this page.

Don Marquis, of the Louisiana Historical Center and the Louisiana State Museum, made available many documents collected for an ambitious exhibit he prepared for the museum in 1989. I drew heavily on the comprehensive jazz archives at Tulane and Rutgers Universities. Curtis Jerde, who administered the William Ransom Hogan Jazz Archive at Tulane, and members of his staff, particularly Richard B. Allen, Alma Williams, and Bruce Raeburn, were most helpful. I am especially grateful to Dan Morgenstern at Rutgers, who allowed me limitless access to the files, including numerous letters, the original typescript to *Satchmo: My Life in New Orleans*, and the Armstrong manuscripts identified here as *Goffin*. He also helped with photo captions. But my debt to Dan goes far beyond that; his writings on Armstrong—a diaspora of liner notes and fugitive articles waiting to be bound in a book—are among the most sensitive and perceptive we have. I am also indebted to Jack Bradley, whose deep love of Armstrong comes through in his many photographs. His collection of Armstrongiana is an inexhaustible treasure.

The generous research assistance of a few friends greatly eased the writing of this book. Mary Cleere Haran, a wonderful singer and actress, is also an experienced and indefatigable researcher who finds documents that elude everyone else; though she performed nightly at the Ballroom, she journeyed to libraries by day and waded through my taped interviews and other materials. Loren Schoenberg, saxophonist, disc jockey, and writer, helped me with interviews and accumulated many hours of material on tape. Will Friedwald helped me assemble the original discography. I would have been hard-pressed without the copying and collating facilities provided me by Norman Halper and his staff at Aaron Halper and Company.

I am delighted to have had the chance to work with Paul Bresnick of Doubleday, who understood what I was trying to do from the beginning, suggested the title (which didn't seem so obvious to me), and steered the book past several obstacles.

I am indebted to those who gave me interviews; to those who responded to a printed query with anecdotes, letters, and pictures; to those who provided other kinds of assistance. They include Milt Gabler, Danny Barker, Jack Bradley, Doc Cheatham, Sallie (Mrs. Trummy) Young, Lassie Joseph, Andrea Young, Milt Hinton, Sy Oliver, Bob Haggart, Joe Wilder, George Chisolm, Richard Gibson, Herb Ellis, Arvell Shaw, Benny Carter, Bud Freeman, Ruby Braff, Kenny Davern, Marty Napoleon, Jean Bach, Barbara Carroll, Barbara Lea, William E. Hassan, Harold S. Kaye, Charles Graham, George T. Simon, Johnny Simmen, Francis J. Walsh, Julius Rosen, Stan Wheeler, Ella Merkel DiCarlo, Norma M. Murchio, Archie Smith, Ed Berger, Martin Williams, Lou Jacobs, Bessie Williams, Gail Hightower, Eugene Kramer, Sam Perlman, Don Hunstein, Jay Emery, Jaynie Botsford, Dodie Simmons, Jesse Bryant, Arlene Kerstetter, Harty Parsons, Fred

Danzig, Roman Zaharchuk, Jerry Czajkowski, Alan Angele, Peter Kirchoff, Anna Beverwijk, Robert Barger, and, of course, Lucille Armstrong.

The contribution of my wife, Deborah Eve Halper, to this book and everything else I do transcends a page of acknowledgments. But I point out her help in collating thousands of documents; her forbearance when I disappeared into my office for several weeks to write the text; her editorial advice; her enthusiasm; her inspiration. Best of all, a year later she gave us Lea.

—G. G.
1988/2000

Index

Africa, 125

"Ain't Misbehavin'," 86, 91

Albert, Mary (a.k.a. Mayann), 22–23,
   25–26, 27–28, 29–30, 32–33, 34,
   36–37, 42, 51

Alexander, Charlie, 97

Alix, May, 51

Allen, Henry ("Red"), 43, 113, 155

"All of Me," 101–102

All Stars band, 124–125
   "Hello, Dolly!" recording, 142–143
   recordings with Kapp Records, 143
   Smith College concert, 139–140
   typical concert with, 133–135
   Trummy Young and, 140

Amadee, Larry, letter to Armstrong,
   151–160

American Humor (Rourke), 7

Anderson, Jean, 74

Anderson, Tom, 42, 158

Apollo Theater, 110

Arkansas, civil rights controversies,
   127–128

Armstrong, Beatrice ("Mama Lucy"), 30,
   34, 36–37, 112

Armstrong, Josephine, 22

Armstrong, Louis
   Larry Amadee's letter to, 151–160

Lucille Armstrong and, 106, 114–116,
   117–118, 119–120

autobiographical writings, xvii–xx

birth date, 21–25

boycotts of, 128

character of, 3–4, 16–17, 138–140

childhood, 22–23, 25–27, 28–40,
   151–152

civil rights and political controversies,
   126, 127–129, 130–132

Johnny Collins and, 95, 97, 100, 102,
   103, 105

Bing Crosby and, 68

draft registration, 22, 23–25

Gil Evans and, 141

FBI file on, 129–130

female singers with, 134–135

film appearances, 9, 94, 110, 121, 125,
   138, 143

Lil Hardin and, 50–52, 54, 59, 60, 96,
   105

heart attacks, 140–141, 150

herbal laxatives and, 30–31

invitation to the White House, 132

King assassination and, 130

later illness and death, 148, 149–150

letters of, xvi, 46–47, 149–150

magazine pieces by, xvi

Mardi Gras of 1949, 131–132
marijuana and, xvii, xviii, 95–96, 107
mobsters and, 97–100
as musician/entertainer: in Africa,
    125; All Stars band, 122, 124–125,
    133–135; with big bands, 91; in
    California, 93–97; with Carroll
    Dickinson, 74–75; in Chicago, 44,
    45–47, 48–52, 59–70, 73–78, 84,
    154–155; with Clarence Williams
    Blue Five, 55; at Connie's Inn,
    86–87; contributions to and impact
    on jazz, 6–7, 52–53, 61–62; at
    Cotton Club, Culver City, 93–94;
    at Dreamland Cafe, 59; early years
    in New Orleans, 23, 41–44; Joe
    Glaser and, 25, 67, 68, 86,
    105–107, 108–109, 121, 125, 148;
    Benny Goodman and, 140; with
    Fletcher Henderson, 52, 53–54;
    humor of, 7–8, 10, 138–139;
    integrated bands and, 82; jazz
    critics on, 83–84; at Newport Jazz
    Festivals, 126–127, 148–149; in
    New York, 52, 53–57, 84–88; with
    King Oliver, 25, 44, 45–46, 48; at
    Sunset Cafe, 67, 68; with Erskine
    Tate at the Vendome, 59–61, 67;
    television appearances, 126, 129,
    142; tours in England and Europe,
    102, 103; Town Hall concert, 122,
    124; unfavorable perceptions of, 4,
    120, 135–136
nicknames, xv, 41
Daisy Parker and, 23, 42
recordings, 161–173; of 1929, 87–88,
    91; of 1930, 94–95; of 1931,
    100–102; of 1932, 102–103; with
    Dave Brubeck, 141; with Columbia
    and Verve, 137; concert albums
    with the All Stars, 125; with Decca
    Records, 109, 110–114, 137–138;
    early collaborations, 48, 55–57;
    with Duke Ellington, 141; Joe
    Glaser and, 136–137, 138; "Hello,
    Dolly!," 141, 142–143; Hot 5 band,
62–67, 75–78; Hot 7 band, 68–70;
    later years, 145–147, 148, 150
residence and domestic life in Corona,
    Queens, 117–120
Bill Robinson and, 8–9, 49–50
seventieth birthday, 148–149
as singer, 4–5, 6; "All of Me,"
    101–102; debut recording, 54;
    Decca recordings, 111; "Hello,
    Dolly!," 4–5; "I Surrender Dear,"
    101; "Mame," 143; scat singing, 54,
    63–64, 67; Rudy Vallee on, 91–92
slang and, 47
Alpha Smith and, 60, 67–68, 96, 105
tape collection of, 118–119
at the Vatican, 138
on white racism, 31–32
writing skills, xvi
Armstrong, Lucille, xix, 86, 95, 127,
    128
    beginning of relationship with Louis,
    114–116
    destruction of Louis's writings, xviii
    on Louis's anger, 140
    residence and domestic life in Corona,
    Queens, 117–118, 120
Armstrong, Mary. *See* Albert, Mary
Armstrong, William, 22, 29, 40
At Pasadena, 125
At Symphony Hall, 125
At the Crescendo, 125
Avakian, George, 137

"Baby, It's Cold Outside," 135
Bach, Jean, 110
"Back O' Town Blues," 135
Bailey, Buster, 53, 54
"Ballad of Davy Crockett, The," 147
Bankhead, Tallulah, xvi, 69
Barbarin, Isadore, 46
Barbarin, Paul, 46, 113, 156
"Barber Shops" (Armstrong), xix
Barcelona, Danny, 135
Barker, Danny, 112, 140
Barnes, Meelie, 156
Baseball team, 100
"Basin Street Blues," 77, 103, 145

Beatles, The, 4
"Beau Koo Jack," 77
Beavers, Louis, 137, 138
Bebop, 120
Bechet, Sidney, 38, 55
Beiderbecke, Bix, 43
Benny, Black, 156, 157
Berigan, Bunny, 111
Bernstein, Leonard, 123
Berry, Chuck, 6
Berton, Vic, 95
Betty Boop cartoons, 101
"Between the Devil and the Deep Blue
    Sea," 101
"Bibbidi-Bobbidi-Boo," 147
Bigard, Barney, 124, 134, 156
"Birth of the Blues," 126
Bishop, Jim, 128
Black, Charles L., Jr., 17
Black, Clarence, 74
"Black and Blue," 14, 92, 125
"Blue Again," 101
"Blueberry Hill," 125, 135
"Blue Monk," 57
"Blue Turning Gray Over You," 15, 137
"Blue Yodel No. 9," 94
Boatner, Edward, 112
"Body and Soul," 15, 95
Bolden, Buddy, 31, 152
Bolton, Red Happy, 156
Boone, Lester, 97
"Boppenpoof Song, The," 120
Boutte (LA), 28, 29
Bradley, Jack, xvii–xviii, 106, 107, 132,
    139, 141
Braud, Wellman, 43
Brickay, Red, 153
Brick House, 42
Briggs, Peter, 69, 74
Brooks, Percy, xv
Brown, Jewell, 134
Brown, Lawrence, 93
Brubeck, Dave and Iola, 141
"Buddy's Habits," 48
Bye Bye Birdie, 141

"Cake Walking Babies from Home," 55,
    62
"Can't Help Lovin' Dat Man," 134
Cara, Mancy, 74, 75
Carmichael, Hoagy, 11, 124
Carroll, Barbara, 107, 108
Carroll, Diahann, 130
Catlett, Sid, 102, 112, 113, 124, 135
Celestin, Papa, 153–154
"Changeable Daddy," 57
"Chattanooga Stomp," 48
Cheatham, Doc, 60–61
Chilton, John, xvi, 95
"Chim Chim Cher-ee," 147
"Chimes Blues," 48
"Chinatown," 101
Chocolate Dandies, 66
Christian, Lillie Delk, 56, 75, 126
Civil rights, Armstrong and, 126,
    127–129, 130–131
Clarence Williams Blue Five, 55
Cliburn, Van, 129
Cole, Cozy, 124, 133
Collier, James Lincoln, 4, 21–22, 24
Collins, Johnny, 95, 97, 100, 102, 103,
    105
Collins, Lee, 155
Colored Waif's Home for Boys, 38–40,
    152
Columbia Records, 137
Condon, Eddie, 87
Connie's Inn, 86–87, 93, 97, 99
Cook, Louise, 86
Co-operative Hall, 43
"Copenhagen," 53
"Cornet Chop Suey," 11, 62, 64–65
Cotton Club (Culver City), 93–94
Cox, Baby, 66
"Creator Has a Master Plan, The," 146
Creole Jazz Band, 45–46, 48, 154–155
Creoles, 28
Crosby, Bing, xii, 5, 6, 68, 95, 110, 126
Crosby, Gary, 110–111
Curry, Bert, 74

Darensbourg, Joe, 143
Davis, Miles, 6, 67, 135, 141

Davis, Peter, 39–40
Davis, Sammy, Jr., 128, 130
Debussy, Claude, 81–82
Decca Records, 109, 110–114, 120,
    137–138
Desvigne, Sidney, 153
Dickerson, Carroll, 74–75, 84, 93
"Dinah," 89
Discography, 161–173. *See also*
    Armstrong, Louis, recordings
Disney Songs the Satchmo Way, 147
Dodds, Baby, 43, 45, 47, 69, 70, 154, 156
Dodds, Johnny, 43, 45, 62, 66–67, 69,
    154, 156
Domino, Fats, 125
"Don't Forget to Mess Around," 11
Dorsey, Tommy, 138–139
"Do You Know What It Means to Miss
    New Orleans," 121
Dreamland Cafe, 51, 59
Dunn, Blind Willie. *See* Lang, Eddie
Durand, Maurice, 155, 160
Dutrey, Honore, 43, 45, 154

Edwards, Eddie, 28
Eisenhower, Dwight D., 127, 128
Elgar, Charles, 74
Elkins, Leon, 93, 94
Ellington, Duke, 108, 132
Ellison, Ralph, 92
Emerson, Ralph Waldo, xx
Erlanger Theater, 49
Esquire, 148
Eureka Jazz Band, 148–149
Europe, James Reese, 24
Evans, Gil, 101, 141
"Everybody Loves My Baby," 53, 55, 62
"Ev'ntide," 111
Ex-Flame, 94

Faubus, Orval, 127, 128
Federal Bureau of Investigation, 129–130
Ferguson, Otis, 94
Fernandez, Butsey, 158
Fitzgerald, Ella, 110, 126, 127, 137
Foster, Frankie, 98–99
Foster, Pops, 43, 113

Francis, Albert, 156
"Froggy Moore," 48
Funky Butt Hall, 31

Gabler, Milt, 121, 137–138
Garcia, Russ, 137
Garland, Joe, 113
Garment, Leonard, 132
Garner, Erroll, 138–139
George V, 101
Gerlach, Horace, xvii
Germany, 136
Ghana, 125
Gillespie, Dizzy, 94, 120–121, 148
"Give Peace a Chance," 146
Glaser, Joe, 119, 127
    Armstrong's career and, 25, 67, 68,
        105–107, 108, 109, 121, 125, 141
    Armstrong's recordings and, 136–137,
        138
    Armstrong's writings and, xvii, xviii
    death of, 109, 148
    integrated bands and, 82
    other clients of, 108
    personality of, 107–108
    relationship with Armstrong, 86, 105,
        108–109
    Jack Ruby and, 130
    Sunset Cafe and, 67, 68
Glenn Miller Story, The, 138
Glenn, Tyree, 124, 135
"God Bless America," 139–140
Goddard, Chris, 90
Goffin, Robert, xviii
"Going to Shout All over God's
    Heaven," 112
Golden Dragon, 100
"Go Long Mule," 53
Gonsoulin, Bertha, 45
Goodman, Benny, 6, 91, 140
Good Morning, Vietnam, 5
Gordon, Dexter, 121
Granz, Norman, 137
Great Day, 86
Green, Zeno, 159–160
Grinnell College, 17
Gross, Paul, 158

"Gully Low Blues," 69
"Gut Bucket Blues," 63

Hackett, Bobby, 124, 139, 140, 148–149
Haggart, Bobby, 137
Haggin, B. H., 83–84
Hall, Edmond, 122, 124
Hall, Tubby Fred, 97, 157
Hampton, Lionel, 94, 95
Handy, W. C., 137
Hardin, Lil (a.k.a. Lil Armstrong), 11,
    45, 50–52, 54, 59, 60, 62, 96, 105,
    154
Harris, Aaron, 158
Hassan, William, 108
Hawkins, Coleman, 53
"Heah Me Talkin' to Ya?," 77
"Heebie Jeebies," 62, 63–64
"Heigh-Ho," 147
Hello, Dolly! (film), 143
"Hello, Dolly!" (song), xii, 4–5, 111, 134,
    141–143
"Hello, Louis" (song), 143
Henderson, Fletcher, 44, 52, 53–54, 59,
    62
Herbal laxatives, 30–31
"He's a Son of the South," 103
Higginbotham, J. C., 113
"High Society," 95
Hill, Alex, 77
Hill, Bertha, 56
Hines, Earl, 64, 68, 73, 74, 75–78, 124
Hinton, Milt, 124–125, 133
"His Father Wore Long Hair," 146
Hite, Les, 94
Hobson, Homer, 74
Holiday, Billie, 108, 110, 121
Holmes, Charlie, 113
Hoover, J. Edgar, 130
Hot Chocolates, 86, 102
Hot 5 (band)
    collaboration with Lonnie Johnson,
        66–67
    with Earl Hines, 75–78
    members of, 62
    recordings, 62, 63–65
    with Don Redman, 77–78

Hot 4 (band), 56
Hot 7 (band), 68–70
"Hotter Than That," 15, 66–67
"How High the Moon," 135

"I Ain't Gonna Tell Nobody," 48
"I Ain't Got Nobody," 70
"I Can't Give You Anything But Love,"
    87–88
"I Double Dare You," 111
"If I Could Be with You," 95
"I Gotta Right to Sing the Blues," 103
"(I'll Be Glad When You're Dead) You
    Rascal You," 101
"I'm a Ding Dong Daddy," 94
"I'm a Little Blackbird," 55
"I'm Confessin'," 94–95, 120–121, 135
Immerman, Connie, 99, 102
"I'm Not Rough," 66
"I'm Putting All My Eggs in One
    Basket," 111, 137
"Indiana," 133, 134, 145
"Indian Cradle Song," 86
Invisible Man (Ellison), 92
"I Surrender, Dear," 101
"I Will Wait for You," 146–147
"I Wish I Could Shimmy Like My Sister
    Kate," 11

Jackson, Mahalia, 149
Jackson, Preston, 97
Jackson, Willi, 158
Jacobs, Phoebe, xviii
Jane Alley, 22, 26, 30
Jazz
    Armstrong as ambassador of,
        82–83
    Armstrong's contributions to and
        impact on, 6–7, 52–53, 61–62
    Leonard Bernstein on, 123
Jazz critics, on Armstrong's music, 4,
    83–84
Johnson, Bill, 45, 154
Johnson, Budd, 102
Johnson, Lonnie, 66–67, 87
Johnson, Margaret, 57
Johnson, Willie ("Bunk"), 38, 152

Jolson, Al, 5, 95
Jones, David, 43
Jones, Joseph, 38–39
Jones, Max, xvi, 139
Jordan, Louis, 102–103
"Jubilee," 111
"Just You, Just Me," 134

Kapp, Jack, 109, 110, 112
Kapp Records, 142, 143
Karnofsky family, 34–36, 37, 38
Kelly, Chris, 155
Kelly, Guy, 155
Kenna's Hall, 31
Kennedy, John F., assassination, 139–140
Keno, Bob, 158
Keppard, Freddie, 45, 51, 155
Kimball, Andrew, 153
King, Larry, 130–131
King, Martin Luther, Jr., 130
"Kiss to Build a Dream On, A," 125, 134
"Knockin' a Jug," 87
Kolodin, Irving, 92–93
Kyle, Billy, 106, 124, 134

Lacosso, Pete, 156
Lang, Eddie, 66
"Laughin' Louie," 12, 103
"La Vie en Rose," 135
"Lazy River," 12, 101, 135
Lee, Thomas, 23, 37
Lincoln Gardens Cafe, 45, 154–155
Lindsey, John, 97, 157
Liston, Virginia, 55
Lombardo, Guy, 87
"Lonesome Weary Blues," 56
Lopez, Vincent, 92
Lorillard Company, 150
"Lot of Livin' to Do, A," 141, 142
Louis, Joe, 155
"Louis Armstrong and the Jewish Family in New Orleans, La. The Year of 1907" (Armstrong), xix
Louis Armstrong Foundation, 28
Louis Armstrong's 50 Hot Choruses for Cornet, 70–71

Louis Armstrong's 125 Jazz Breaks for Cornet, 70–71
"Lover, Come Back to Me," 134
"Low Land Blues," 56
Lynn Murray Choir, 111

"Mabel's Dream," 48
"Mack the Knife," 125, 135, 145
Madden, Owney, 99
Madison, Bingie, 113
"Mahogany Hall Stomp," 87, 101
"Make Me a Pallet on the Floor," 137
Mama Lucy. *See* Armstrong, Beatrice
"Mame," xii, 143
Marable, Fate, 23, 42–43, 156
Ma Rainey and Her Georgian Jazz Band, 55
Mardi Gras, 131–132
Marijuana, xvii, xviii, 95–96, 107
Massenet, Jules, 81–82
Matranga, Henry, 24
Mayann. *See* Albert, Mary
McRae, Teddy, 121
"Melancholy," 70
"Melancholy Baby," 129
Melody Maker, 136
Melrose Bros. Music Company, 70
"Memories of You," 95, 134
Merrick, David, 141, 143
Middleton, Velma, 14, 125, 126, 134–135
Miller, Punch, 155
Mills Brothers, 110
Milne Municipal Boys Home, 39. *See also* Colored Waif's Home for Boys
Monk, Thelonious, 57
"Mooche, The," 66
"Mood Indigo," 146
Moore, Morris, 158
"Mop Mop," 135
Morgan, Sam, 155
Morgenstern, Dan, xi, xvii, 92
Morton, Jelly Roll, 69
Mugging, 89–90
"Muggles," 76–77, 96
Murphy, George, 129
"Muskrat Ramble," 5, 11, 62, 63, 64, 145
"My Bucket's Got a Hole in It," 15, 134

"My Heart," 63
Myles, Isaac, 29, 32–33
"My One and Only Love," 146
"My Sweet," 95

Napoleon, Marty, 18
"Negroe Neighborhood" (Armstrong), xix, 25–26
Nelms, Chris, 136
Nelson, Louis, 156
New Orleans
    Armstrong's birth and childhood in, 22–23, 25–27, 29–30, 31–32, 34–40, 151–152
    Armstrong's early career in, 23, 41–44
    honky-tonks and dance halls, 31, 157–158
    Mardi Gras of 1949, 131–132
    musicians from, 152–154, 155–158
    reminiscences by Armstrong and Amadee, 151–154, 156–160
"New Orleans" (Armstrong), xix
New Orleans, 121
Newport Jazz Festival, 126–127, 148–149
Nicholas, Albert, 113, 155, 156
Nicholas, Wooden Joe, 155
"Night Before Christmas, The," 150
Nkrumah, Kwame, 125
"No Blues," 67
Noone, Jimmie, 74, 140

"Oh, By Jingo!," 64
OKeh Records, 84
    Hot 5 recordings, 62–67
    Hot 7 recordings, 68–70
"Ole Miss," 134
Oliver, Joe, "King Oliver," 77
    in Chicago, 25, 44, 45–46, 48, 154–155
    death and burial of, 155–156
    Joe Glaser and, 108
    idolized by Armstrong, 38, 154
    in New Orleans, 23, 152, 153, 156–157, 158
    Luis Russell and, 113
Oliver, Sy, 137, 138
"One of These Days," 53

On Her Majesty's Secret Service, 148
Onward Brass Band, 153
"Oriental Strut," 64
"Ornithology," 135
Ory, Kid, 11, 23, 43, 44, 62, 69

"Papa De-Da-Da," 55
Parker, Charlie, 52
Parker, Daisy, 23, 42
Paul VI, 138
Pennies from Heaven, 110, 111
"Perdido," 134
Perez, Manuel, 153
Persson, Bent, 70–71
Peterson, Oscar, 137
Petit, Buddy, 153
Peyton, Joseph L., 39
"Pickin' on Your Baby," 55
Poitier, Sidney, 130
Pollack, Ben, 87
Porgy and Bess, 137, 141
"Potato Head Blues," 5, 69
Powell, Adam Clayton, 128
Powers, Ollie, 51
Présence Africaine, 129
Prima, Louis, 101
Private Lives, 69

Rabell, Fred, 54
Rainey, Ma, 55
Randolph, Zilner, 97
Rangel, Charles, 132
Rap music, 112
Real Ambassadors, The, 141
Redman, Don, 53, 77–78
Rena, Kid, 152
Republican Party, 132
Rhapsody in Black and Blue, 9
"Riverside Blues," 48
Robichaux, John, 153
Robinson, Bill ("Bojangles"), xix, 8–9, 49–50
Robinson, Fred, 74, 75
"Rockin' Chair," 124, 135
Rockwell, Tommy, 84, 85–86, 87, 93, 95, 97, 99, 102
Rodgers, Jimmie, 94
Rolfe, B. A., 92

Roseland Ballroom, 53
Rourke, Constance, 7
Ruby, Jack, 130
Russell, Luis, 87, 113
"Russian Lullabye," 36

St. Cyr, Johnny, 43, 62
"St. James Infirmary," 77
"St. Louis Blues," 62, 145
"Saints, The," 135
"Salt Peanuts," 94
"Samba de Orpheus," 65
Satchmo: My Life in New Orleans
    (Armstrong), xvii–xviii, 32
Satchmo (album), 137–138
Satchmo the Great (film), 125
"Save It Pretty Mama," 77
Savoy Ballroom, 74, 84
"Savoy Blues," 66
Scat singing
    Armstrong's debut with, 54
    in "Heebie Jeebies," 63–64
    in "Hotter That That," 67
Schiff, Dr. Alexander, 18, 149, 150
Schuller, Gunther, 75
"Second Hand Rose," 55
"Shanghai Shuffle," 53
Shaw, Arvell, 125, 133, 135
"Shine," 9, 94
Showboat club, 97
Shu, Eddie, 134
Sinatra, Frank, 126, 143
Singleton, Zutty, 73, 74, 75, 84, 85, 156
"Skeleton in the Closet," 111
"Skip the Gutter," 77
"Sleepy Time Down South," 100–101,
    133, 134, 135, 145
Smiley, Bob, 116
Smith, Alpha, 60, 67–68, 96, 105
Smith, Bessie, 56, 62
Smith, Clara, 56
Smith College, 139–140
"Snake Rag," 48
"S.O.L. Blues," 69
"Someday," 135
"Song of the Vipers," 103
"Special Delivery Blues," 57

Spirituals, 112
Stacy, Jess, 43
"Stardust," 11–12
Steve Allen Show, The, 129
Stewart, Jimmy, 138
Stoptime, 64
Storyville, 23, 31
Streckfus, Joseph, 42
Strip, The, 125
Strong, Jimmy, 74, 75
"Struttin' with Some Barbecue," 11, 65,
    112, 145
Suburban Gardens, 100
"Sugar Foot Stomp," 62
"Sunny Side of the Street," 103
Sunset Cafe, 67, 68, 73
"Sunshine Baby," 57
"Super Tiger Rag," 103
"Sweetheart on Parade," 95
Swing, 53
Swing That Music (Armstrong), xvii,
    91–92
"Swing That Music" (song), 112
Swiss Kriss, 139
Sydney, S. S., 42, 43

"Taint What You Do, It's the Way That
    You Do It," 11
"Talk to the Animals," 147
Tallerie, Pierre, 127
Tate, Erskine, 59–61, 88
Taylor, Eva, 55, 57
Teagarden, Jack, 43, 87, 124, 135
"Tears," 48
"Tenderly," 137
"Thanks a Million," 111
"That's My Desire," 135
"That's My Home," 103
Theile, Bob, 141
"Them There Eyes," 63
Thomas, Hersal, 56–57
Thomas, John, 69, 70
Thomas, Leon, 146
Thompson, Virgil, 6
"Tiger Rag," 66, 134
"Tight Like That," 77–78
"Too Busy," 56

Toohey, Rev. J. M., 22
Town Hall concert, 122, 124
Tuxedo Brass Band, 42, 154
Tuxedo Jazz Band, 44
"Twelfth Street Rag," 70

Umbrellas of Cherbourg, The, 146
Usonia dance hall, 74

Valenti, Jack, 130
Vallee, Rudy, 91–92, 101
Vamp, 64
Vatican, 138
Vendome Theater, 59–61, 67, 73
Verve Records, 137
Victor record company, 102

Wade, Louis Clark, 158
Walker, Catherine, 22
Wallace, Sippie, 56–57
Waller, Fats, 11, 137
Washington, Dinah, 108
Waters, Ethel, 5, 88
Watson, Joe, 156
"Way Down Yonder in New Orleans," 134
"Weary Blues," 69–70
"Weather Bird," 11, 77
"Weather Bird Rag," 77
Webb, Chick, 102
Weill, Kurt, 125
"We Shall Overcome," 146
West Africa, 125.
"West End Blues," xii, 5, 67, 75–76
Westerberg, Hans, 4, 145
Wethington, Crawford, 74

"What a Wonderful World," 5, 146
What's My Line?, 142
"When I Grow Too Old to Dream," 134
"When the Saints Go Marching In," 112, 145
"When You're Smiling," 92–93
"When Your Lover Has Gone," 101
"When You Wish Upon a Star," 147
"Where Did You Stay Last Night?," 48
"Whiffenpoof Song, The," 120
"Whistle While You Work," 147
Whitburn, Joel, 5
White, Lulu, 158
White Citizens Council, 126
Whiteman, Paul, xvii, 68
"Wild Man Blues," 11, 69
Willet, Chappie, 113
Williams, Bert, 7
Williams, Clarence, 55, 62
"Willie the Weeper," 70
Wilson, Lucille. *See* Armstrong, Lucille
Wilson, Teddy, 102
"Wolverine Blues," 112

"Yes I'm in the Barrel," 63
"You Are My Lucky Star," 111
"You Can't Shush Katie," 57
Young, Sallie, 106
Young, Trummy, 11, 124, 135, 140, 143
"You Rascal You," 9
"You've Got Me Voodoo'd," 112
"You Won't Be Satisfied," 110

Zucker, Dr. Gary, 149, 150